New Directions for
Student Services

John H. Schuh
EDITOR-IN-CHIEF

Elizabeth J. Whitt
ASSOCIATE EDITOR

Gambling
on Campus

George S. McClellan
Thomas W. Hardy
Jim Caswell
EDITORS

Number 113 • Spring 2006
Jossey-Bass
San Francisco

GAMBLING ON CAMPUS
George S. McClellan, Thomas W. Hardy, Jim Caswell (eds.)
New Directions for Student Services, no. 113
John H. Schuh, Editor-in-Chief
Elizabeth J. Whitt, Associate Editor

NEW DIRECTIONS FOR STUDENT SERVICES (ISSN 0164-7970, e-ISSN 1536-0695) is part of The Jossey-Bass Higher and Adult Education Series and is published quarterly by Wiley Subscription Services, Inc., A Wiley Company, at Jossey-Bass, 989 Market Street, San Francisco, California 94103-1741. Periodicals Postage Paid at San Francisco, California, and at additional mailing offices. POSTMASTER: Send address changes to New Directions for Student Services, Jossey-Bass, 989 Market Street, San Francisco, California 94103-1741.

New Directions for Student Services is indexed in College Student Personnel Abstracts and Contents Pages in Education.

Microfilm copies of issues and articles are available in 16mm and 35mm, as well as microfiche in 105mm, through University Microfilms Inc., 300 North Zeeb Road, Ann Arbor, Michigan 48106-1346.

SUBSCRIPTIONS cost $75 for individuals and $180 for institutions, agencies, and libraries. See ordering information page at end of book.

EDITORIAL CORRESPONDENCE should be sent to the Editor-in-Chief, John H. Schuh, N 243 Lagomarcino Hall, Iowa State University, Ames, Iowa 50011.

www.josseybass.com

CONTENTS

FOREWORD

It was in 1999 when Sheldon (Shelley) Steinbach, of the American Council on Education (ACE), asked me what NASPA was doing in regard to gambling among college students. Shortly after this, McKinley (Mack) Boston, then the vice president for student development and athletics at the University of Minnesota, pulled me aside at a meeting to tell me that gambling among athletes and other college students was becoming a problem that student affairs ought to be addressing. I was stunned to hear that there was a problem. I called on NASPA leaders George S. McClellan, who was then at Northwestern University, and the vice president for student affairs at Southern Methodist University, Jim Caswell, to help in bringing people together who had an interest in looking at this issue in order to see whether or not a significant number of college students were gambling, and if they were, to what extent it was a problem.

George and Jim were cochairs of what became the NASPA National Task Force on College Student Gambling. The task force comprised a university president, vice presidents, directors of residence halls, directors of judicial affairs, directors of public service, leaders of the National Collegiate Athletic Association, a professor of psychiatry, athletic directors, and researchers. Cochairs McClellan and Caswell had their first face-to-face meeting with members of the task force in March 2000 in Seattle. They created a listserv, met via conference calls, and commissioned research to collect data on the habits related to gambling among a sample of college students. Researchers found that many administrators were unwilling to allow their students to be surveyed for fear of what the data might show.

When results from the survey were released in July 2001, skeptics wanted more data and responded to the task force report as if the problem were being manufactured. Others seemed to want to let sleeping dogs lie. It was as if they were thinking that if we don't know anything about this problem, then we don't have to do anything about it. Despite the lack of support and interest from colleagues, cochairs of the task force, in collaboration with the NASPA office, continued to write papers, talk to the media, and present programs at national and regional conferences. A few years later, when I e-mailed George and Jim to ask for their sense of the state of college student gambling and their thoughts on whether or not NASPA ought to continue its activities and outreach in this area, George wrote, "I'm afraid the genie

NEW DIRECTIONS FOR STUDENT SERVICES, no. 113, Spring 2006 © Wiley Periodicals, Inc.
Published online in Wiley InterScience (www.interscience.wiley.com) • DOI: 10.1002/ss.189

is out of the bottle." Jim concurred by cautioning, "I really think this issue will soon overwhelm us in the college and university environment."

Today, gambling has become ubiquitous. There are a riot of gambling-related advertisements, television shows, and Web sites. Legalized gambling takes place in hotel and riverboat casinos, tribal gaming casinos, race tracks, bingo halls, charity events, and lotteries. Illegal gambling takes place via the Internet, in rooms around our communities, and on our campuses. Notwithstanding the popularity of the many forms of gambling, poker is one of the hottest sports today. It is not surprising, therefore, to find that so many of our students are engaging in gambling behavior of a number of kinds, at varying levels of intensity, and with disparate impact on their lives and the lives of those around them.

Steven Johnson (2005), writing about what he calls the "sleeper curve," argues that "the landscape of popular culture involves the clash of competing forces: the neurological appetites of the brain, the economics of the culture industry, and changing technological platforms" (p. 10). He tells us that in order to "understand those forces we'll need to draw upon disciplines that don't usually interact with one another: economics, narrative theory, social network analysis, and neuroscience" (p. 11). The forces that Johnson cites are the same elements that are at work in instances of problem gambling.

Keith Whyte, executive director for the National Council on Problem Gambling, says that young people "learn about drugs and alcohol, but nobody is talking to these kids about responsible gambling" (Karp, 2005, p. W4). His comments raise three questions. Why should this be done? How should it be done? Who should do it?

Why should we become involved in addressing campus gambling? We must be concerned about campus gambling for several reasons. First, for many of our students it is an illegal activity either because of their age or because of the venue in which they are gambling. Second, we must be concerned about students who indulge in compulsive behavior where the consequences can be harmful. Third, there are developmental implications and opportunities associated with student gambling behavior. As an aside, although I have spoken here about our concern for students, it is important to note that some of these same concerns can be raised regarding members of our staff and faculty.

How should we set about addressing campus gambling? We live among a generation of gamers, and gambling is a powerful outlet for their hunger and fascination. To think that the issues associated with college gambling will dissipate on their own or that a traditional campus awareness campaign is sufficient to influence behavior change among students who are at risk of becoming problem gamblers is to delude ourselves and shortchange students. As with mental health problems, underage drinking, smoking, and unprotected sex, just giving students information or asking them to refrain or abstain does not usually work. Education and intervention efforts must be based on research. They must be comprehensive and collaborative. They must include students as stakeholders and active participants. Finally, they must be assessed with regard to efficacy.

Who should address campus gambling? It is the responsibility of students, parents, student affairs professionals, coaches, faculty, members of the gaming industry, and professional and sports associations all doing our share to become informed and speak to the problem. Student affairs professionals are well situated to take the initiative in raising awareness about campus gambling and in pulling together the necessary campus and community coalitions to address the issue.

This volume is an important addition to the literature because it offers elemental information regarding college gambling, shares ideas for action and research, and challenges us to become actively and intentionally engaged in addressing campus gambling and its implications for our students and our campus communities. I encourage readers to use this book as a helpful primer as we address campus gambling. Read and share this book as acknowledgment of the problem and as our pledge to explore and find ways to work together to address all the elements of this complex trend. Learn from the research, meet with colleagues, create working groups, use the existing structures within associations such as knowledge communities, divisions, and commissions to begin the hard work of rooting out information about how our students are spending their time.

We cannot throw up our hands because the genie is out of the bottle. We must not become overwhelmed by the size of the problem, and we must not remain ignorant of the issue; to do so can seriously impede the current and future success of students.

References

Johnson, S. *Everything Bad Is Good for You: How Today's Popular Culture Is Actually Making Us Smarter.* New York: Riverhead Books, 2005.
Karp, H. "The Senior Trip to the Strip." *Wall Street Journal,* Apr. 8, 2005, p. W4.

GWENDOLYN JORDAN DUNGY *is executive director of the National Association of Student Personnel Administrators.*

EDITORS' NOTES

We hope that this volume of *New Directions for Student Services* is useful as a sourcebook on campus gambling for student affairs professionals, student affairs graduate students and graduate preparation program faculty, counseling and health education professionals working in a college setting or with college students, and others in higher education. We also hope that the volume serves as a resource for campuses wishing to be proactive addressing campus gambling, and for those campuses that find themselves in the unfortunate position of needing to react to challenges presented as a result of campus gambling.

The volume opens with Gwendolyn Jordan Dungy's challenge, in the Foreword, to student affairs professionals and others concerned with student success in college to become better informed regarding campus gambling and be actively involved in education and intervention efforts.

The first five chapters are an effort to provide historical and contemporary information regarding campus gambling. In Chapter One, George S. McClellan and Ken C. Winters offer an overview of information related to gambling, including the links between higher education and gambling. Chapter Two, written by Jim Caswell, gives readers a glimpse into the student perspective regarding campus gambling. The next three chapters address some of the hottest trends in campus gambling: Tom W. Hardy discusses the current poker craze and its impact on college campuses in Chapter Three, sports wagering is the focus of Donald L. Rockey, Jr., and Chris King in Chapter Four, and Stuart J. Brown shares information related to Internet wagering in Chapter Five.

Chapter Six, written by Randy Stinchfield, William E. Hanson, and Douglas H. Olson, summarizes information related to problem and pathological gambling on the part of college students. We are hopeful that this chapter will be of particular interest to counseling and health education professionals working with college students, but we are confident that the information in the chapter is valuable for our broader audience as well.

The next two chapters are focused on campus preparedness with regard to gambling. In Chapter Seven, Jason A. Laker offers a discussion of important ethical and practical considerations in promoting campus preparedness. In contrast to Laker's more theoretical consideration of the issue, Chris King and Tom W. Hardy describe in Chapter Eight an existing campus model for a gambling education and intervention program.

In the final chapter, we as coeditors offer a summary of the recurring messages from the volume as well as a few closing thoughts of our own. We

NEW DIRECTIONS FOR STUDENT SERVICES, no. 113, Spring 2006 © Wiley Periodicals, Inc.
Published online in Wiley InterScience (www.interscience.wiley.com) • DOI: 10.1002/ss.190

5

conclude with a list of resources through which readers can explore additional and more detailed information regarding various aspects of the campus gambling issue.

We are grateful to the authors who have contributed their work to this volume. Their knowledge about campus gambling and their concern for the welfare of college students, college communities, and colleges as institutions of higher education is evident in the quality of their contributions. We are also grateful to John Schuh and Liz Whitt for their decision to include a volume on campus gambling as part of the *New Directions in Student Services* series and for their invaluable editorial support. Finally, we are grateful to our students, colleagues, friends, and families for their support throughout the development of this volume. A special note of thanks goes to Roberta Kudrna, an associate of George McClellan's, for her invaluable administrative support throughout this project. Whatever success this volume has in achieving its goals is the result of the contributions of all these people. Any shortcomings are ours and ours alone.

The three of us also want to publicly acknowledge the National Association of Student Personnel Administrators, including its executive director, Gwendolyn Jordan Dungy, for the work that the association has done in the area of campus gambling. Over the past decade NASPA has convened its Gambling Task Force, monitored developments in campus gambling and public policy related to campus gambling, and furnished information about campus gambling to practitioners through a variety of sources (including conference presentations, a white paper, and a Web site). We are proud to be part of the student affairs professional association that, more than any other, has offered leadership on this issue.

As coeditors, the three of us came to this project with varying experiences and perspectives related to campus gambling. However, we were and continue to be unanimous on several key points regarding the issue. First, our work in this volume is intended to raise awareness about campus gambling, promote reflection and discussion among student affairs professionals and others in higher education about the issue, and encourage research and the scholarship of practice in this area. Second, although we do not presume to have all the answers, we are hopeful that we have surfaced the important questions. Finally, any determination with regard to our success in attaining these goals rests with our readers.

George S. McClellan
Tom W. Hardy
Jim Caswell
Editors

GEORGE S. MCCLELLAN is vice president for student development at Dickinson State University; he served as lead author of NASPA's white paper on campus gambling and was cochair of NASPA's Gambling Task Force.

THOMAS W. HARDY is director of housing and residence life at Valdosta State University and previously served as cochair of the Gambling Action Team at the University of Alabama.

JIM CASWELL is vice president for student affairs at Southern Methodist University. He served as coauthor of NASPA's white paper on campus gambling and was cochair of NASPA's Gambling Task Force.

1

Gambling is a part of human history, and it is currently enjoying unparalleled popularity around the world. This chapter gives a brief definition and history of gambling, information about the rate of participation by college students, and suggestions for practice and future research.

Gambling: An Old School New Wave Challenge for Higher Education in the Twenty-First Century

George S. McClellan, Ken C. Winters

"If you bet on a horse, that's gambling," said Blackie Sherwood, a well-known sportswriter. "If you bet you can make three spades, that's entertainment. If you bet cotton will go up three points, that's business. See the difference?" (in Urbanowicz, 1998, p. 1).

Evidence suggests that gambling is as old as the human race and has been a part of many of the great cultures in human history (GamblingPhd. com, 2003; Reith and Ferguson, 2002). Throughout that history, the attitude of people and their governments toward gambling has been marked by ambivalence. The expansion of gambling was at times evolutionary and at other times revolutionary, and along the way there were periods of time of contraction in gambling as the result of public backlash (Dunstan, 1997; GamblingPhd.com, 2003). As this volume is being prepared, gambling is in a period of rapid expansion worldwide that has lasted for over two decades.

Whether this period of gambling expansion continues at its current pace, dwindles, or even contracts to some extent, it is important to note that throughout the lives of the current generation of young adults and their younger peers gambling has been legal, socially acceptable, and increasingly popular as a recreational activity (Shaffer, Hall, Vander Bilt, and George, 2003). It is not surprising, therefore, to find that young people around the world are engaging in gambling behavior at a significant rate (International Center for Youth Gambling Problems and High-Risk Behaviors, 2001).

NEW DIRECTIONS FOR STUDENT SERVICES, no. 113, Spring 2006 © Wiley Periodicals, Inc.
Published online in Wiley InterScience (www.interscience.wiley.com) • DOI: 10.1002/ss.191

Given the extent to which young people are engaging in gambling behavior, it is important for all of us who work with and care about college students to be informed about gambling, the extent to which students are participating in it, and the potential implications of gambling behavior for students and for our campus communities. This chapter provides an overview of that information. Although the emphasis throughout is on information available regarding gambling and gambling behavior in the United States, we hope the information will also be useful to colleagues in Australia (Colman and Colman, 2005), Canada (Adebayo, 1995), South Africa (Harvard Medical School, 2001), and elsewhere around the world who share in supporting student success and who are facing similar challenges related to campus gambling behavior.

The chapter begins with an explanation of the various ways in which gambling can be defined. It then moves to a short history of gambling in the United States, followed by discussion of the historical links between gambling and education (particularly higher education) in the country. Information is then laid out regarding the scope of gambling behavior, the extent of such behavior among college students, and the types of gambling in which students most frequently engage. The chapter concludes with recommendations for practice and research and a few summary comments.

Defining Gambling

Gamble means "1a: to play a game for money or property, b: to bet on an uncertain outcome," or "2: to stake something on a contingency: take a chance" (Mish, 2005). However, as demonstrated by the words of Blackie Sherwood that opened this chapter, defining and understanding gambling requires moving beyond the dictionary. In this section of the chapter, we describe it in a variety of ways. First, we define gambling by enumerating types of gambling activity. Second, we add a discussion of legality to our understanding of what constitutes gambling. The final element in this chapter's development of a definition of gambling is discussion of the venues in which gambling occurs.

Types of Activity. One way of defining gambling is by describing the various types of activities constituting gambling. The four major types of gambling activities are pari-mutuel betting, lotteries, casino gaming, and charitable gaming (Eadington and Cornelius, 1991).

Pari-mutuel Betting. In pari-mutuel gambling, the gamblers are essentially wagering against one another, and the odds for the wagers are a function (at least in part if not in sum) of the distribution of the total dollars wagered over the set of betting options available. The total prize pool is made up of the amount bet on all options less a percentage for the operator of the game. One example of pari-mutuel gambling is wagering on horse or dog races. Another is sports betting.

Lotteries. Lotteries are similar to pari-mutuel betting in that the total prize pool is made up of the amount bet less a percentage held by the operator of the game. Lotteries differ from pari-mutuel gambling in that the odds of selecting a winning option are determined by the structure of the game rather than by the wagering patterns of the other players of the game. Keno is an example of lottery gambling.

Casino Gaming. The defining characteristic of casino gambling is that the players are wagering against the operator. Casino operators make money by only offering games that have a long-term expected positive result for the operator. An individual player might make money in the short run, but the casino operator expects to make money by extending the duration of play and maximizing the volume of play of the gamblers in its games. Popular casino gambling games include slot machines, blackjack, and craps.

Charitable Gaming. Charitable gambling may encompass any of the other three types of gambling activity, but it is distinguished from the others in that the gambling activity is being run for the benefit of a nonprofit organization. Even though charitable gaming is gambling that benefits a charity, it is sometimes the case that the game or games being offered to benefit a particular charity are run by a for-profit management entity. The ambivalence that some feel toward other forms of gambling is mediated when the same activity benefits a charity (Imam-Muhni, 1993; King, 1985). Examples of charitable gaming are state lotteries, church bingo, raffles for student organization travel, and poker nights for athletic fundraising.

Legality. In addition to describing types of gambling activity, gambling may also be defined as a matter of law. In the United States, the authority to legalize and regulate gambling rests with state and local governments, tribal governments, and the federal government. As a result of the complexity of jurisdictional intersections, the compelling nature of the economic and social issues at stake, and the rapidly changing nature of the underlying enterprise, gambling law is somewhat unsettled and constantly evolving (Humphrey, 2005; Jarvis and others, 2003).

Once legalized, the authority to regulate gambling is typically delegated by the state or tribal government to an agency of that government. Assuming that gambling is permitted within a particular state or tribal nation, there are typically several variables taken into account by the governing authority in defining which activities constitute legal gambling (Humphrey, 2005):

- The role of skill versus chance in the outcome of the game
- Whether or not the host of the game earns money as a host beyond what might be earned as a player in the game
- Whether or not Internet gambling is expressly prohibited

The steady expansion of gambling has coincided with an ongoing debate regarding the question of what age a young person should attain before being allowed to gamble. It is not a surprise that legal limitations based on age exist for gambling. Perhaps what is surprising about the issue of age limits in this country is that a uniform minimum age does not exist for all forms of gambling. Whereas the federal government has stepped in and directed states to establish uniform age limits for purchasing tobacco products (age eighteen) and alcohol (age twenty-one), it has stayed on the sideline regarding an age limit for gambling. The legal age for gambling in the United States varies by state and, at least in some states, by type of game. Rose (2003) presents a detailed summary of legal age and gambling for each state. Interestingly, there are no data to support the contention that young people who have easier access to casino-style gambling have a higher rate of problem gambling than do youths without such access.

Given the local and complex nature of gambling laws and regulations, it is important to note that nothing in this section is intended to constitute legal advice or opinion regarding specific circumstance or issues. Readers are encouraged to consult appropriate counsel should they be in need of advice or interpretation regarding a gambling-related matter on their campus.

Venue. Another way of defining gambling is by categorizing the venues in which the activity takes place. There are three primary types of venues for gambling: bricks-and-mortar, or real world; phone or other electronic media; and the Internet.

Bricks and Mortar. Currently, eleven states have 445 commercial casinos. In 2004, the commercial casinos in the United States generated almost $29 billion. An additional $19.4 billion was produced in 376 of the 405 tribal casinos located in twenty-eight states (Ritter, 2005; Walton, 2005). It is impossible to determine with any certainty the number of illegal or less formal bricks-and-mortar gambling venues or the amount of money that changes hands in them.

Tribal gambling is an interesting and rapidly growing sector of the bricks-and-mortar gambling industry in the United States. Through the Indian Gaming Regulatory Act of 1988, the federal government recognized the authority of sovereign tribal nations to establish and operate gambling enterprises on tribal land (Humphrey, 2005; Hills, 2004).

Phone or Other Electronic Media. Options for interstate legal gambling via the phone or other electronic media are limited as they are prohibited by the Interstate Wire Act of 1961. Some states (such as Pennsylvania and New York) do allow phone accounts for in-state pari-mutuel wagering. As is the case with bricks-and-mortar gambling, it is difficult to determine the amount of illegal gambling activity that takes place via phone and other electronic media.

Internet. The third venue for gambling is the Internet, and it is the one in which there is currently the greatest growth. The more than two thousand Internet gambling sites took in almost $10 billion in 2004, making gambling one of the largest sectors of e-commerce (Swartz, 2005). This is particularly remarkable when it is noted that the majority of the revenue from online gambling comes from clients in the United States, where the legality of online gambling is arguably an area of law as yet unsettled (see Brown's Chapter Five for a more complete discussion on this point).

History of Gambling

I. Nelson Rose (as cited in Dunstan, 1997), a scholar in gambling studies, has described the history of gambling in the United States as consisting of three waves. Each is discussed in this section, and a fourth wave is then identified and discussed as well.

The First Wave. Rose describes the first wave as beginning during the colonial period and extending to the midnineteenth century. All of the colonies used lotteries to help fund themselves. Some of the proceeds were used by the colonies to establish their institutions of higher learning. The first of the lotteries in the colonies was established on Long Island by the midseventeenth century, and casinos serving the more affluent Americans were established by the early nineteenth century. It was during the first wave that gambling flourished in the southern states, particularly in areas where waterways and ports served as a center for economic activity. As the first wave of gambling came to a close in the United States, antigambling forces were holding sway as the result of religious concerns and backlash stemming from gambling-related scandals (Dunstan, 1997).

The Second Wave. The second wave as described by Rose began just after the conclusion of the Civil War and continued through the early years of the twentieth century. Gambling moved west during this time as the country expanded in that direction and people poured into California pursuing gold. New Orleans was supplanted by San Francisco as the hub of gambling activity in the United States. Gambling had become so integrated into the American culture at this point that gambling and gamblers feature prominently in the works of some of the nation's great novelists of the time (Reed, 2004). The second wave was much shorter in duration than the first, but it too ended with antigambling forces at play as a result of legal challenges to gambling and backlash stemming from gambling fraud (Dunstan, 1997).

The Third Wave. The third wave of gambling in the United States began during the Great Depression. Americans looked to gambling as a way of addressing the financial hardships they faced, particularly following the 1929 crash of the stock market (Dunstan, 1997). By the close of the 1930s, twenty-one states had legalized race tracks, and low-stakes charity bingo spread throughout the nation. During the decades of the 1940s and 1950s, nearly every state had legalized pari-mutuel wagering and low-stakes gambling for charitable purposes (Rose, 1997).

Legal state-sponsored lotteries ended in 1894, but illegal lotteries continued to flourish. In 1964 New Jersey became the first state with a legal state-sponsored lottery in the twentieth century. Several states followed suit, but rapid expansion of state-sponsored lotteries marked the 1970s and 1980s, when states faced mounting pressure to fund education, health care, and other social programs while dealing with stiff opposition to tax increases (Dunstan, 1997).

In 1931, Nevada (which had rescinded legal gambling just two decades earlier) became the first state in the twentieth century to legalize casino gambling. It would be a number of years before, fueled by infusions of capital from pension funds and corporate interests, Las Vegas would become a national attraction (Von Herrmann, 1997). Atlantic City's first casino opened in 1978, and riverboat gambling was legalized in the early 1990s in Illinois, Iowa, and Mississippi. By the late 1990s, twenty-five states and three territories legalized casino gambling in one form or another (Rose, 1997).

A Fourth Wave. Rose described three waves of gambling in the United States (Dunstan, 1997). We suggest that a fourth wave exists. This latest wave, which began in the late 1990s, is defined by the accelerated growth of commercial casinos in several states, rapid expansion of tribally controlled gambling, and the explosion of gambling on the Internet fueled by improved technology, greater confidence in the integrity of online casinos, and the popularity of poker (Swartz, 2005). The fourth wave continues to the present day and shows no signs of abating any time soon.

Gambling and Higher Education

Having discussed the history of gambling in the United States, we turn to the historical and current connections between gambling and higher education. Among the connections discussed are funding, mission, college sports, and college students.

Funding. Gambling and higher education have been linked from the earliest days of the American colonies. All of the colonies had lotteries that helped fund a variety of public services, and proceeds from those lotteries served to establish Harvard, Yale, Columbia, Dartmouth, Princeton, and William and Mary (Dunstan, 1977). By the Civil War, the establishment of fifty colleges had been at least partially funded by lottery revenues (North American Association of State and Provincial Lotteries, 2005). As higher education enrollments expanded in the last three decades of the twentieth century and strictures on state funding mounted, gambling proceeds were once again a common source of funding for higher education—and, in a more modern development, for scholarships to support students attending higher education institutions (Adams, 1995; Bazinsky, 1993; Overland, 2005; Sack, 2004).

Mission. Today higher education is linked to gambling in each of higher education's three historical missions: teaching, research, and service.

Teaching. A growing number of institutions offer courses in casino management:

- For professional development or certification (see, for example, the programs at the University of Nevada Reno; http://extendedstudies.unr.edu/gaming.htm)
- As part of an associate degree program in casino management (see the Three Rivers Community College program; http://www.trcc.commnet.edu/Prog_Study/Business/Hosp_Prog_Study.htm)
- As part of larger hospitality management baccalaureate degree programs (see the University of Massachusetts at Amherst's program; https://www.umassulearn.net/ProgUGradBSHRTA.htm.asp

Tribally controlled colleges have offered associate degree programs in casino management for several years (for example, at Lac Courte Oreilles Ojibwa Community College; http://www.lco-college.edu/). In a particularly interesting development, tribal communities with gambling interests have recently begun to partner with predominantly white institutions to deliver such programs. Tulane University has entered into a relationship with the Choctaw (Associated Press, 2005), and San Diego State University has received a $5.5 million donation from the Sycuan Band of the Kumeyaay Nation for the purpose of establishing a national center for curriculum and research on tribal gaming (San Diego State University, 2005).

Research. The first academic research center to focus on gambling was the Institute for the Study of Gambling and Commercial Gaming (http://www.unr.edu/gaming/index.asp), which was founded in 1989 at the University of Nevada Reno. The University of Nevada Las Vegas hosts a similar center (http://gaming.unlv.edu/), and several institutions have academic centers devoted to problem or pathological gambling. Among these are Harvard University (http://www.hms.harvard.edu/doa/institute/index.htm) and the University of California Los Angeles (http://www.npi.ucla.edu/center/gambling/). Among the scholarly journals publishing gambling-related articles are the *Journal of Gambling Studies* (http://www.ingentaconnect.com/content/klu/jogs) and the *Journal of Gambling Issues* (http://www.camh.net/egambling/).

Service. Training knowledgeable and skilled casino staff and undertaking research that may be used, among other purposes, to enhance profitability through enhanced marketing, operating, or political strategies are arguably all service functions carried out by higher education for the gambling industry. In addition, it is increasingly common in certain areas of the country for a campus to afford campus access to employers in the gambling industry for recruitment of staff.

College Sports. There are many ways in which higher education and gambling are linked, but it is likely that the first connection many people would make between higher education and gambling is related to collegiate athletics. Issues related to gambling on college athletics (Tucci, 2004; Wheeler, 2001) and gambling by athletes (NCAA, 2003; Whelan, 1992) are an unfortunate part of the history of American higher education (see Chapter Four, by Rockey and King, for a more complete discussion of this issues).

College Students. The historical link between college students and gambling parallels the financial link between their institutions and gambling. Shaffer (2003) notes that young people have always been attracted to gambling and further observes that a variety of forms of gambling have been popular with youth throughout the twentieth century. In the modern era—the fourth wave described earlier—gambling is actively marketed to college students by gambling interests. The modern gambling industry clearly sees young people (notably college students) as an important part of their market now and in the future (Woodyard, 2004). Nowhere is this clearer than in efforts to promote and extend the current craze in poker. Poker interests are recruiting campus representatives (CardPlayer.com's program; http://www.cardplayer.com/campus_rep/). Announcers on televised poker tournaments appear to make it a point to note that certain players at a final table are students (or in some cases were students until they dropped out to play poker) and are now gambling for substantial potential winnings. There is even an online College Poker Championship with free entry that offers scholarships and donations to charity as prizes. In 2005, that event attracted twenty-five thousand students from around the world and was won by a junior from the University of Minnesota (CollegePokerChampionship.com, 2005; Krieger, 2005; Poker777.com, 2005).

Prevalence

Having noted the history of college student involvement in gambling, we feel it is instructive to summarize the scope of gambling by college students across two domains: gambling involvement and the severity of the gambling problem. Because there are now a wealth of prevalence studies on gambling behavior in the United States, several reviews have been published. We draw on the two most recent and rigorous of these: the Harvard meta-analysis (Shaffer, Hall, and Vander Bilt, 1997) and the summary by the National Research Council (1999). The Harvard report included sixteen study samples; the National Research Council report, which had more stringent inclusion criteria, included fourteen of the sixteen Harvard study samples in its report. As can be expected, the findings from the two reports are concordant on all major conclusions, although the two reports differ to some degree in the amount of detail reported.

Gambling Involvement. There is almost a universal finding among gambling prevalence studies that gambling by college students is relatively common, and a select group of games tend to be favored by this group. The

**Table 1.1. Prevalence of Gambling Activity by Age Group, Based on
Meta-Analysis**

Game	College (%)	Adolescents (%)	Adults (%)
Casino games	61	13	15
Lottery	60	30	49
Noncasino card games	36	40	16
Sports gambling	31	31	15
Games of skill	24	32	10
Pari-mutuel	9	11	7
Financial markets	4	—	6

Notes: Adapted from Harvard meta-analysis (Shaffer, Hunt, and Vander Bilt, 1997), p. 47, Table 15.

Number of study samples from which the meta-analysis was based: college, 15; adolescents, 22; adults, 50.

Harvard meta-analysis reported that the lifetime prevalence rate of gambling for college students was 85 percent, compared to 81 percent for adults and 78 percent for adolescents (Shaffer, Hall, and Vander Bilt, 1997). Thus, on this level, college students gamble more frequently than other general age groups. Of course, the lifetime prevalence figure represents only a general estimate of gambling involvement. It is not a direct indication of gambling frequency or intensity, nor of amount wagered or lost. Whereas such detailed data pertaining to gambling involvement is not available at the national level, we will return to this issue of how college students compare to other age groups when we discuss gambling problem severity.

Both the Harvard and NRC reports identified a subset of games that were commonly played by college students. We turn to the Harvard report for the most detailed data on this issue. Table 1.1 summarizes these data; we include the findings for adults and adolescents for comparative purposes.

The four most prevalent games for college students were (average rate in parentheses) casino games (61 percent), lottery (60 percent), card playing (not at a casino; 36 percent), and sports gambling (31 percent). A ranking of the lifetime prevalence rate by game produces a similar list. Of course, these averages are partially dependent on cohort factors. The Harvard college studies represent studies from the late 1980s to the mid-1990s. It is interesting to speculate how recent technology and cultural trends may alter the ranking of prevalence of gambling activity. For example, card playing by current college students may be higher than the average in prior years given the rapid growth in popularity of Texas Hold 'Em poker and the media attention surrounding national poker tournaments. Also, online gambling allows easy access for nearly everyone to all kinds of high-stake games. Another issue is due to the expansion of casino gambling in America: more college students are within close proximity of a casino than in the recent past. Indeed, proximity to casinos has been shown to be related to frequency of gambling involvement (Korn and Shaffer, 1999), including for college students (Hardy, 2002).

Gambling Problem Severity. Whereas the published literature has referred to severe end gamblers with various terms (for instance, problem gamblers, compulsive gamblers), the official term from a psychiatric nomenclature perspective is "pathological gambling." The DSM-IV criteria characterize pathological gambling in relatively precise terms (National Research Council, 1999), yet that use as a basis to define gambling severity for youth is controversial because it was developed from adult-based research (Shaffer, Hall, and Vander Bilt, 1997), and rigorous validity evaluations of the criteria for youths are lacking (see Derevensky, Gupta, and Winters, 2003).

An intriguing alternative to the DSM-IV system—intriguing in part because it has features that are relevant to the youth gambling debate—was proposed by Shaffer and Hall (1996). This classification system distinguishes various levels of gambling problem severity. Level zero includes those who have never gambled; level one is for individuals who have gambled but are not experiencing any gambling-related problems. Level two gamblers, or so-called at-risk gamblers, reflect those who are experiencing some problems related to gambling but at a subclinical level. Level two gamblers are presumed to be experiencing a few (less than five) of the DSM-IV symptoms of pathological gambling. Level three gamblers are those individuals who meet formal criteria of pathological gambling, such as experiencing five or more DSM-IV symptoms of pathological gambling. The Shaffer and Hall classification system has several advantages, particularly from a developmental standpoint. For one, it consists of two intermediate categories (level one, nonproblem gamblers; level two, at-risk gamblers), both of which are likely to be highly relevant when characterizing college gamblers. Also, the level two category offers a conceptual basis for studying the developmental transitions from less severe to more severe forms of gambling involvement. Finally, the classification system retains the pathological gambling concept (level four). This standard of definition of severe-end gambling problems—despite its potential problems when applied to youth—is still used by countless other researchers, including those who are testing its validity in young people.

Similar to the gambling involvement data, college students also show high rates of Level 2 and Level 3 gambling compared to other age groups. Both the National Research Council and Harvard reports yield detailed data here, but we focus on the findings from the Harvard report given that it entailed more comparison. As summarized in Table 1.2, the average rate of lifetime level two and level three gambling by college students is 7 percent and 5 percent, respectively. These rates are much higher than the findings from the adult studies yet are generally in line with the adolescent rates. (For past year rates, there were insufficient data for the college group, so our discussion here is limited to lifetime rate.)

Table 1.2. Prevalence Estimates of Problem Gambling by Age Group, Based on Meta-Analysis

Disorder Group	College (%)	Adolescents (%)	Adults (%)
Level two, lifetime	7.0	8.6	3.4
Level three, lifetime	5.1	4.3	1.7

Note: Source is Harvard meta-analysis (Shaffer, Hall, and Vander Bilt, 1997), p. 38, Table 8. Level two and Level three designations are based on studies that used the original South Oaks Gambling Screen (SOGS; Lesieur and Blume, 1987).

The three age groups can be more precisely compared with the relative risk statistic. A relative risk represents the risk of one group having a condition (say, level three) compared to another or reference group's risk of having the same condition. When the adult group is assigned as the reference group, the relative risk that a college student will experience a lifetime level three gambling disorder is 2.9; for adolescents it is 2.4 (Shaffer, Hall, and Vander Bilt, 1997). Thus, on the basis of the studies reviewed by the Harvard group, college students are nearly three times more likely to have already experienced a level three gambling disorder compared to adults (see the chapter by Stinchfield, Hanson, and Olson later in this volume for a comprehensive discussion).

Conclusion

Gambling has been associated with higher education in a variety of ways throughout the history of the United States, and the college years appear to be a vulnerable time associated with increased gambling and problem gambling. Entry to college for many students signifies increased freedom, more disposable income, and the opportunity to legally gamble at many sites or venues. The expanding legalization and promotion of gaming in the last decade has produced a parallel upsurge in the prevalence rates of lifetime, past-year, and problem gambling among youth, including college students (Ladouceur, Boudreault, Jacques, and Vitaro, 1999). The majority of college students gamble, and some exhibit symptoms of problem gambling (level two or level three).

Student affairs professionals and others concerned with supporting the success of college students and of institutions of higher education must become familiar with information and issues related to the impact of gambling on college campuses. Attention should be given to developing education and intervention practices, assessing the effectiveness of these programs, and sharing information regarding best practices.

One significant area for future research is better understanding of the individual and environmental factors associated with college gambling.

Recent research has emphasized the biopsychosocial approach to understanding the factors that contribute to the onset and maintenance of gambling behaviors (Shaffer and Kidman, 2003). Whereas there have been several cross-sectional studies on the correlates of psychosocial factors and gambling involvement on the part of adolescents (Stinchfield and Winters, 1998), there is less empirical work with respect to the influence of mediating and moderating factors on college student gambling behavior. Given the prominence of social life in a college setting, it is likely that many college students are motivated to gamble for social reasons (Neighbors, 2002), but personality characteristics, such as disinhibition, may influence college gambling behavior as well (Winters, Bengston, Dorr, and Stinchfield, 1998).

Another area of need for future research is related to the health service delivery issues that arise once a college student has a problem with gambling. The troubling prevalence rate of problem gambling and the potential social and personal harm associated with severe-end gambling have led one national expert to recommend that all college students be screened for potential problems with gambling (Lesieur and others, 1991). At minimum, a college student reporting level two or level three gambling behavior should trigger a comprehensive assessment and possible referral to treatment. More research is needed to refine and validate this screening and assessment process, and what types of treatment are feasible within college student health systems.

In 1976, the Commission on the Review of National Policy Toward Gambling noted, "Gambling is inevitable. No matter what is said or done by advocates or opponents of gambling in all its various forms, it is an activity that is practiced, or tacitly endorsed, by a substantial majority of Americans" (p. 1). The continued growth of gambling in the quarter century hence lends ample evidence that the gambling genie is not going back in the bottle.

References

Adams, H. G. "Perceptions of Upper Level Higher Education Administrators and Legislative Officials in Alabama Concerning the Fiscal Management and Funding of Four-Year Public Colleges Within the Higher Education System of Alabama." Dissertation Abstracts International, 1995, vol. 57.

Adebayo, B. Gambling Among College Students: Extent and Social Characteristics. Lac La Biche, Alberta: Office of Research and Development, Alberta Vocational College, 1995.

Associated Press. "Tulane Gambling on Indian Casino." July 24, 2005. http://www.ledger-enquirer.com/mld/ledgerenquirer/news/local/12213368.htm; accessed July 24, 2005.

Bazinsky, J. M. "A Comparison of Florida Legislators' and Public Community College Administrators' Opinions Regarding Selected Funding Sources for Public Community Colleges." Dissertation Abstracts International, 1993, vol. 55.

CollegePokerChampionship.com. "The 3rd Annual College Poker Championship." 2005. http://www.collegepokerchampionship.com/; accessed July 20, 2005.

Colman, R., and Colman, A. "Adolescent Gambling in the ACT." *Youth Studies Australia,* 2005, *24,* 7–8.

Commission on the Review of the National Policy Toward Gambling. *Gambling in America.* Washington, D.C.: GPO, 1976.

Derevensky, J., Gupta, R., and Winters, K. C. "Prevalence Rates of Youth Gambling: Are the Current Rates Inflated?" *Journal of Gambling Studies,* 2003, *19,* 405–426.

Dunstan, R. "Gambling in California." California Research Bureau. 1997. http://www. library.ca.gov/CRB/97/03/crb97003.html; accessed July 8, 2005.

Eadington, W. R., and Cornelius, J. A. (eds.). *Gambling and Public Policy: International Perspectives.* Reno: Institute for the Study of Gambling and Commercial Gaming, University of Nevada, 1991.

GamblingPhd.com. "The History of Gambling." 2003. http://www.gamblingphd.com/ historical-information.htm; accessed July 24, 2005.

Hardy, T. W. "A Comparative Examination of the Casino Gambling Habits of College Students in Four Southeastern Higher Education Institutions: Implications for Higher Education Decision-Makers." *Dissertation Abstracts International,* 2002, vol. 63.

Harvard Medical School. "The Gambling Attitude of South African University Students: A Cross-Continental Perspective." *Wager,* 2001, *6.* www.wager.org; accessed Nov. 6, 2001.

Hills, C. "History of American Indian Law and Gambling." Family.org. 2004. http://www.family.org/cforum/fosi/gambling/gitus/a0030889.cfm; accessed July 18, 2005.

Humphrey, C. "Gambling Laws US." 2005. http://www.gambling-law-us.com; accessed July 5, 2005.

Imam-Muhni, D. "'Charitable Gambling' in American Culture: An Ethnographic Study of Bingo and Poker Players." *Dissertation Abstracts International,* 1993, vol. 55.

Indian Gaming Regulatory Act, 25 U.S.C. § 2719 (1988).

International Center for Youth Gambling Problems and High-Risk Behaviors. *The Second International Think Tank on Youth Gambling Issues Summary Report.* Montreal, Quebec: McGill University, 2001.

Interstate Wire Act, 18 U.S.C. § 1084 (1961).

Jarvis, R. M., Bybee Jr., S. L., Cochran, J. W., Rose, I. N., and Rychlak, R. J. *Gaming Law Cases and Materials.* New York: LexisNexus, 2003.

King, K. M. "Gambling for God: Charity and Self-Interest in the Bingo Parlor." *Dissertation Abstracts International,* 1985, vol. 47.

Korn, D., and Shaffer, H. "Gambling and the Health of the Public: Adopting a Public Health Perspective." *Journal of Gambling Studies,* 1999, *15,* 289–365.

Krieger, L. "The College Poker Championship, Where Cash Scholarships and Charitable Donations Are Won at the Poker Table." *Card Player Magazine,* 2005, *17.* http://www.cardplayer.com/poker_magazine/archives/showarticle.php?a_id=14058and m_id=65537; accessed July 20, 2005.

Ladouceur, R., Boudreault, N., Jacques, C., and Vitaro, F. "Pathological Gambling and Related Problems Among Adolescents." *Journal of Child and Adolescent Substance Abuse,* 1999, *8,* 55–68.

Lesieur, H. R., Cross, J., Frank, M., Welch, M., White, C. M., Rubenstein, G., Mosely, K., and Mark, M. "Gambling and Pathological Gambling Among University Students." *Addictive Behaviors,* 1991, *16,* 517–527.

Mish, F. C. *Merriam-Webster Online Dictionary.* 2005. http://www.m-w.com/cgi-bin/dictionary?book=Dictionaryandva=gambling; accessed July 24, 2005.

National Collegiate Athletic Association (NCAA). *2003 National NCAA Study on Collegiate Sports Wagering and Associated Behaviors.* Indianapolis, Ind.: NCAA, 2003.

National Research Council. *Pathological Gambling: A Critical Review*. Washington, D.C.: National Academy Press, 1999.

Neighbors, C. "Exploring College Student Gambling Motivation." *Journal of Gambling Studies*, 2002, *18*, 361–370.

North American Association of State and Provincial Lotteries. "Lottery History." 2005. http://www.naspl.org/history.html; accessed July 18, 2005.

Overland, M. A. "Jackpot for Higher Education." *Chronicle of Higher Education*, July 1, 2005, p. A7.

Poker777.com. "Chad Flood Named Best College Poker Player at Online Poker Championship." 2005. http://www.poker777.com/20050609/chad-flood-named-best-college-poker-player-at-online-poker-championship_1725_ocfihr.php; accessed July 20, 2005.

Reed, N. "High-Stakes Citizenship: Gambling in the American Novel, 1890–1929 (Mark Twain, Edith Wharton, F. Scott Fitzgerald)." *Dissertation Abstracts International*, 2004, vol. 65.

Reith, G., and Ferguson, H. *The Age of Chance: Gambling in Western Culture*. New York: Routledge, 2002.

Ritter, K. "Commission Reports Tribal Casinos Earned $19.4 Billion in 2004." *Las Vegas Sun*, July 14, 2005. http://www.lasvegassun.com/sunbin/stories/nevada/2005/jul/14/071410236.html; accessed July 14, 2005.

Rose, I. N. "Gambling and the Law: Pivotal Dates." *Public Broadcasting Service*. 1997. http://www.pbs.org/wgbh/pages/frontline/shows/gamble/etc/cron.html; accessed July 27, 2005.

Rose, I. N. "Underage Gambling and the Law." In H. J. Shaffer, M. N. Hall, J. Vander Bilt, and E. M. George (eds.), *Futures at Stake: Youth, Gambling, and Society*. Reno: University of Nevada Press, 2003.

Sack, J. L. "HOPE Scholarships Contribute to Enrollment Surge." *Education Week*, Oct. 6, 2004, p. 24.

San Diego State University. "Sycuan Donates $5.5 Million to SDSU to Create Nation's First Tribal Gaming-Focused Institute." July 25, 2005. http://advancement.sdsu.edu/marcomm/news/releases/spring2005/pr072505.html; accessed July 27, 2005.

Shaffer, H. J. "The Emergence of Gambling Among Youth: The Prevalence of Underage Lottery Use and the Impact of Gambling." In H. J. Shaffer, M. N. Hall, J. Vander Bilt, and E. M. George (eds.), *Futures at Stake: Youth, Gambling, and Society*. Reno: University of Nevada Press, 2003.

Shaffer, H. J., and Hall, M. "Estimating the Prevalence of Adolescent Gambling Disorders: A Quantitative Synthesis and Guide Toward Standard Gambling Nomenclature." *Journal of Gambling Studies*, 1996, *12*, 193–214.

Shaffer, H. J., Hall, M. N., and Vander Bilt, J. *Estimating the Prevalence of Disordered Gambling Behavior in the United States and Canada: A Meta-Analysis*. Boston: Harvard Medical School, 1997.

Shaffer, H. J., Hall, M. N., Vander Bilt, J., and George, E. *Futures at Stake: Youth, Gambling, and Society*. Reno: University of Nevada Press, 2003.

Shaffer, H. J., and Kidman, R. "Shifting Perspectives on Gambling and Addiction." *Journal of Gambling Studies*, 2003, *19*, 1–6.

Stinchfield, R. D., and Winters, K. C. "Adolescent Gambling: A Review of Prevalence, Risk Factors and Health Implications." *Annals of American Academy of Political and Social Science*, Mar. 1998, *556*, 172–185.

Swartz, J. "Online Gambling Sites Expect Big Payoffs." *USA Today*, Feb. 7, 2005. http://www.usatoday.com/money/industries/technology/2005–02–07-gamble-usat_x.htm; accessed Feb. 16, 2005.

Tucci, D. C. "Athletic Reform in Higher Education: Faculty Athletic Representative's Perspectives." *Dissertation Abstracts International*, 2004, vol. 65.

Urbanowicz, C. F. "Gambling in the United States of America from an Anthropological Perspective." Paper presented at the Fourteenth International Congress of Anthropological and Ethnological Sciences, Williamsburg, Va., July 1998.

Von Herrmann, D. K. "The State's Biggest Gamble: Are Competition and Public Opinion Shaping American State Gambling Policy? (Alabama, Illinois, Louisiana, New Jersey)." *Dissertation Abstracts International,* 1997, vol. 59.

Walton, M. "The Business of Gambling." *Cable News Network.* July 6, 2005. http://www.cnn.com/2005/US/07/06/cnn25.top25.gambling; accessed July 6, 2005.

Wheeler, J. "Professor's Book Looks at Sports Betting in America." *NevadaNews,* Oct. 9, 2001. http://www.unr.edu/nevadanews/detail.aspx?id=114; accessed July 20, 2005.

Whelan, D. C. "Organized Crime, Sports Gambling and Role Conflict Victimization and Point-Shaving in College Basketball." *Dissertation Abstracts International,* 1992, vol. 54.

Winters, K. C., Bengston, P., Dorr, D., and Stinchfield, R. D. "Prevalence and Risk Factors of Problem Gambling Among College Students." *Psychology of Addictive Behaviors,* 1998, *12,* 127–135.

Woodyard, C. "Casinos Struggle to Find Way to Deal in Next Generation." *USA Today,* Nov. 8, 2004. http://search.epnet.com/login.aspx?direct=trueanddb=aphandan=J0E306270047404; accessed July 15, 2005.

GEORGE S. MCCLELLAN *is vice president for student development at Dickinson State University; he served as lead author of NASPA's white paper on campus gambling and was cochair of NASPA's Gambling Task Force.*

KEN C. WINTERS *is director of the Center for Adolescent Substance Abuse Research and a professor in the Department of Psychiatry at the University of Minnesota.*

2

This chapter explores students' perspectives regarding campus gambling by listening to their gambling-related experiences and stories. Similarly, the chapter presents the perspective of a senior student affairs officer regarding campus gambling.

Listening to Their Stories: Students' Perspectives About Campus Gambling

Jim Caswell

For more than ten years as a senior student affairs officer, I have been concerned about the growing involvement of students on my campus in the gambling craze that is affecting our society. Along with others in our field, including my friend and colleague George McClellan, I have tried to gain traction on this issue with colleagues. Those efforts, however, have met with limited success. It is my sense that gambling was a stealth concern among many of my senior student affairs officer colleagues. When I would bring the issue up in conversation, they would often indicate they were aware students were gambling. They would typically also share that, thanks to the press of the many other issues with which they were dealing, addressing campus gambling was not a priority unless the issue somehow became very visible on their campus.

Recently, two phenomena occurred that appear to be raising the visibility of campus gambling on many campuses. The first of these is the explosion of Internet gambling by students (see Stuart Brown's Chapter Five for a more thorough discussion). The second phenomenon is the astounding surge in the popularity of poker as college students' gambling game of choice. Readers should see the next chapter, by Tom Hardy, for more information about the poker craze on college campuses.

These two phenomena were recently brought home on my campus when David Williams, one of our students, won a second-place prize of $3.5 million in the World Series of Poker Tournament in Las Vegas. His notoriety forced me to look more closely at the experiences of students on our

NEW DIRECTIONS FOR STUDENT SERVICES, no. 113, Spring 2006 © Wiley Periodicals, Inc.
Published online in Wiley InterScience (www.interscience.wiley.com) • DOI: 10.1002/ss.192

campus with gambling and to explore more in depth whether or not SMU had a gambling problem.

David's story is not atypical of many students. He started playing poker as a teenager and soon found himself reading rulebooks and strategy books on poker and playing often. He entered the 2004 World Series of Poker Tournament with $10,000 he had made from smaller poker tournaments and online gambling. After winning $3.5 million, he continues to enter major poker tournaments and is referred to as "the college kid" in tournaments he enters (Gonzales, 2004).

Because of my continued interest in campus gambling issues, the explosion of Internet gambling and poker, and the impact of the David Williams story on my own campus, a staff member and I surveyed more than six hundred students at my institution in the spring of 2005. The intent of the survey (which is in the appendix) was to elicit student perspectives regarding campus gambling. Their stories are shared in this chapter. Next, thoughts from a recently submitted student paper on gambling and from an interview with a campus student leader are presented. The chapter concludes with some of my own thoughts regarding what I learned from the student stories and the implications those stories may have for the work with students that others are doing on their campuses.

Student Voices from the Survey

Although I plan to focus primarily on the qualitative aspects of students' stories in response to the survey question, it might be helpful to first relate some broad quantitative generalizations. In large part the generalized findings are consistent with the existing literature on college student participation in gambling (see Chapter One by McClellan and Winters for a review of that literature).

Quantitative Generalizations. In our survey, there did not appear to be one particular type of student who gambled. They were Greek and non-Greek, athletes and nonathletes, persons of faith and not, involved and uninvolved, students of all racial and ethnic backgrounds, and students affiliated with a variety of organizations, all gambling in a variety of gaming activities. Students who did not gamble were equally varied.

The majority of students responding to the survey who said they gambled indicated that they participated in card games as their primary form of gambling. Further, they indicated poker (Texas Hold 'Em and straight poker) and blackjack were their games of choice. More men than women participated in card games. Slots and horse racing were also listed as favorite gambling activities. Interestingly, one student reported betting on domino games.

The frequency of gambling reported ranged from every day to a few times a year. The majority of the students responding indicated they played either once a week or twice a month. Again, males tended to play more often than females.

The best gambling wins reported ranged from $5 to $600, with an average being $100 for both males and females. The biggest loss reported was also $600, with an average of $40. One male student responded that his largest loss was "Lots!"

Qualitative Aspects. There were clear themes in the response to the question regarding the positive and negative aspects of gambling.

Positive Perspectives. Many of the students who discussed gambling as a positive experience indicated that the games are fun and that gambling is a social activity. Some of the students with a positive perspective saw gambling as a way to make money or be a big winner. There were a variety of additional reasons for gambling, among them the excitement of playing, learning to read people, meeting new friends, making one think, and supporting making positive judgment calls. More than one student identified competition as a positive aspect of gambling. One male commented that playing poker "allows me to beat someone who underestimates me."

A male sophomore theater major indicated he doesn't gamble often, but when he does it is just for fun. He likes the chance to win. Another male said it is social and allows a lot of time and fun with friends. Winning money is a benefit for him.

A female junior who lives in her sorority house and is involved in a lot of student activities stated that she drinks a lot socially and grew up gambling with her friends and family. For her, gambling is just a fun social event. She loves dressing up and then going drinking and gambling. She says it is "cheap thrills" for her. Gambling is really nothing she has ever questioned or thought about and was part of her culture growing up.

A female sophomore, a commuter student, loves Texas Hold 'Em and participates in a weekly tournament with friends. She says it is really just social and gives them something fun to do. It is cheaper than a lot of things a big group could do together and is just fun.

One student would definitely consider himself an avid gambler. Texas Hold 'Em is his game. He gambles very often but says it doesn't have a negative affect on his schoolwork. He gambles mostly for social reasons and just for the pure joy of the game and enhancing his thinking skills. Now that he has gotten good at it, he knows how to play to win money too. He talked a lot about underground poker games. Interestingly, this same student related that he has seen many friends get into trouble, gambling away rent and even being beaten up.

Negative Perspectives. A smaller number of students shared comments reflecting a negative perspective of gambling. Of those students making such comments, most addressed concern regarding loss of control. Specifically, students mentioned worrying about losing too much money, becoming addicted, losing track of reality, or losing their temper. Several female students reported that one reason they did not gamble was they lacked an understanding of the games.

Among the responses from male nongamblers were these:

• To me it has always been a stupid way to lose money. Of course I have bought a few lottery tickets here and there just for fun, but it has never been a thing that I do too often.

• Gambling is a risk I'm not willing to take. The chances of winning are slim and most of the time, money is wasted due to the belief that the more you bet, the greater your chances are of winning . . . when, in reality, it greatly increases the chances of losing. Gambling is a waste of time and money, and a "quick fix" for those otherwise bored with their lives, but just creates more problems in the end. I'd like to save my money for something useful and/or productive.

• I find no joy in it and believe it is rather ridiculous.

• I do not gamble but I have never really thought of it as something that was bad until the Athletic Department had a guest speaker last semester. I'm not gonna lie, it scares me. People really do get sucked into the thrill of winning. It's just as addicting as any drug and I think it's important for everyone to be informed on how dangerous and life-threatening gambling can be.

Here are responses received from female students who reported not gambling:

• I don't want to lose money. I don't know how to play the popular games (e.g., Texas Hold 'Em) and most people that play are really into it and aren't interested in playing with people who don't know how to play or aren't very good. Most people I know that gamble do so quite regularly and often go to bars on Texas Hold 'Em night or play on the Internet a lot. Several guys I know play online daily and often win a lot of money.

• I just don't ever have any money I want to throw out the window. I used to deal blackjack and when we were learning how to deal, we had to play a lot. I couldn't even gamble the fake money. One or two members in my family have had issues with gambling, so I don't want to go down that road.

• I lack the resources in two ways: (1) I haven't the money and (2) I don't really have any friends who gamble much. Also, I have notoriously bad luck in all things.

• No, because it is against my cultural and religious standards and beliefs for young children and even adults to gamble and having grown up in such an environment, have never really been interested in it. I do not know how to and didn't bother to learn.

All of the respondents except one indicated that gambling had no effect on their schoolwork. The one student who responded otherwise indicated that gambling had helped him achieve better grades! Since the survey did not allow follow-up, it is unclear why this student responded in this manner.

From a Paper on Gambling

As part of a course being offered by a colleague, a student recently wrote and submitted a paper on the current college poker craze. Here are a few of the points from the paper, in the student's voice:

> Out of all the dorms on campus, [X] Hall ranks as the number one hot spot for poker games. The hall's reputation as the "party dorm" combined with the latest trend creates a wild combination. The third floor resident assistant said her residents "literally sleep, eat and drink poker. You can come in there at lunchtime and they're playing poker. Come after class and they are playing poker. When I go on rounds at midnight, they are playing poker. It's everywhere, all the time.

She goes on to indicate that the poker game has become the new social event that counters fraternity and sorority parties. The theme of the game is the social aspect of playing for a good time without getting drunk. The thinking part of gambling keeps students returning for more. In addition, students see this social interaction as not only a mind game but also a game of real competition with their friends. The student's paper continues:

> Gambling adds an extra element to poker games. It's fun to gamble. "I get an adrenaline rush every time I bet," admits one student. However, players run the risk of becoming addicted to the "rush" when playing poker. There's a fine line between loving to play poker and being addicted to gambling. The R.A. worries about her residents who constantly play poker. She stated, "I think poker is all fun and games until it controls their lives. When I see a lot of the guys playing every day, I'm scared it might become an addiction."
> A student golfer claims he became addicted to playing poker over the summer. "You get addicted without knowing it," he said. "I definitely was. I kept making the rationalization that it was OK to gamble my money because I was winning."

From an Interview with a Student Leader

In a recent interview I had with a student leader about why students gamble and especially play poker, a few reasons were given:

NEW DIRECTIONS FOR STUDENT SERVICES • DOI 10.1002/ss

- It is a game of chance and is attractive because anyone can win.
- Players want to believe they are good and "the little guy" can make it big.
- One is really "somebody" if only at the game and only for a short time.
- It is a social activity.

As you can see, the voices of the students in the survey responses, the paper, and the interview reflect a common picture regarding students' perspectives of campus gambling. Interestingly, their voices are also reflective of what the literature reveals regarding the reasons for choosing to gamble or not. According to Habib (2005), the primary reasons students choose to gamble are to win money, social contact, excitement, having something to do, and pursuit of intellectual challenge.

Sharing My Own Thoughts and Summing up

In these statements, we see that gambling is a commonplace part of the lives of our students. It is easy for a social activity such as gambling to become an addiction for some students (see the work of Stinchfield, Hanson, and Olson in Chapter Six).

As a senior student affairs officer, hearing these students' voices reinforces for me that campus gambling is an important and growing concern in student life on college campuses. What we learn from these students is that we, as professionals, have more to learn and more work to do.

I am concerned that some student affairs professionals are too accepting of the gambling craze, as evidenced by increased gambling-related programming on college campuses. We justify getting on the poker bandwagon because there is no exchange of money in our gambling programming. For example, the American College Union-International Region Twelve Fall Conference 2005 mailing advertises a Casino Night where "students can win prize money," which can be used to bid at auction for two round-trip tickets to Europe. However, we must consider whether these sponsored activities reinforce actions that can lead to addictive behavior. Jason Laker's Chapter Seven is helpful in challenging us to develop a consistent ethical framework related to campus gambling.

In addition to articulating a coherent and consistent framework from which to address campus gambling, I would like to suggest several other important steps that campuses should take in this area. First, find out what the student perspective of gambling is on your campus. It is clear that we must listen more closely to students to better understand their stories. It is important that we as practitioners do a better job of environmentally scanning our campus through survey and focus groups to better determine next steps. I recommended something simple as a starting point, such as the survey in the appendix. I suspect the survey results will reflect trends in gambling on your campus similar to what was revealed on my own campus.

Second, if the surveys and focus group results warrant next steps, a task force should be developed to pursue a campus response. King and Hardy describe a model for one such program in Chapter Eight. Whatever action is taken, it is important to make a response on your campus that uniquely fits your campus environment.

Third, develop enforcement and educational programs for your campus. The NASPA white paper on college gambling (McClellan and others, 2002) offers a framework for campus preparedness that may be helpful to you in this effort. Student affairs professionals have done a good job of developing enforcement and educational programs for our campuses in the areas of alcohol and drug abuse, sexual assault, and racial insensitivity. It is highly recommended that the same attention be given to the concerns raised regarding student gambling.

As noted in the beginning of this chapter, the explosion of gambling in all of its forms is on us. This is no longer a stealth issue on our campuses. We must listen to our students and focus on their responses as we formulate our next steps. Yes, statistics are helpful, but as a profession we must engage in understanding the gambling phenomenon by listening to and hearing what students are telling us. It is imperative that we do so.

Appendix

2005 Survey, Southern Methodist University

In spring of 2005, a survey was developed and e-mailed to more than six hundred students, mainly at Southern Methodist University but including some students from other universities. The survey is reproduced here.

Name (optional):
Phone (optional):
Age:
Race:
Year:
Male/Female:

1. Do you ever gamble?
   a. If so, please continue questions 2–10.
   b. If not, what are your reasons? Never been interested? You don't think it is worth risking money on chance?
2. What type of gambling have you participated in (internet, casino, cards with friends, lottery, sports bets, etc.)?
3. How often do you play?
4. What is your favorite game, and why?
5. What is your best win?

6. What is your worst loss?
7. Why do you like to play?
8. What are the positive aspects of gambling?
9. What are the negative?
10. What type of effects do you think it has on your schoolwork?
11. Any stories or comments you would like to share?

Would you be available to interview and talk more? If so, what is the best way to contact you?

References

Gonzalez, J. "Dynamite Dave." *Dallas Observer,* July 1, 2004. http://www.dallasob-server.com/issues/2004–07–01/news/feature.html; accessed Oct. 18, 2005.
Habib, D. "Online and Obsessed." *Sports Illustrated,* May 30, 2005, pp. 68–77.
McClellan, G., Caswell, J., Beck, B., Graves-Holladay, C., Mitchell, A., and Wong-O'Connor, K. *Gambling, Its Effects and Prevalence on College Campuses: Implications for Student Affairs.* Washington, D.C.: National Association for Student Personnel Administrators, 2002.

JIM CASWELL is the vice president for student affairs at Southern Methodist University; he served as coauthor of NASPA's white paper on campus gambling and was cochair of NASPA's Gambling Task Force.

3

This chapter explores the proliferation of poker (both live and online) and discusses how campuses have responded to this activity. The chapter concludes with some implications for practice and further research.

A Minute to Learn and a Lifetime to Master: Implications of the Poker Craze for College Campuses

Thomas W. Hardy

"On a typical night online I'll start out with $100. I'll play until I lose. I'll look at the screen, tears in my eyes, and think of all the things that I need money for. So I play again, put in another $100." So says a college junior who has lost more than $100,000 playing poker since his senior year in high school (Walters, 2005). He gambles on average $400 a day playing poker online for twelve hours at a time and disregarding life routines such as eating, having visitors, speaking on the phone, or even using the restroom.

On another campus, one male student admits he kept money intended for textbooks and instead used it for online poker tournaments as well as card games around campus. He is now in debt and behind in some classes. He begs friends for money to play in the hope of getting even.

Another male student on the same campus mentioned spends ten hours a day playing poker and skips a lot of classes because he is too tired from staying up all night playing poker. He mentions the time he is skipping class is also time he can play in a couple of online poker tournaments. He does not feel addicted and says no harm has been done (Gooley, n.d.).

Although most will not take playing to the extremes these students have, many students on our campuses are involved in playing poker, live or online. The behavior may be legal and appropriate for some, and it may be illegal and problematic for others.

NEW DIRECTIONS FOR STUDENT SERVICES, no. 113, Spring 2006 © Wiley Periodicals, Inc.
Published online in Wiley InterScience (www.interscience.wiley.com) • DOI: 10.1002/ss.193

This chapter opens with information about poker and about the current popularity of poker. The wide access to the game enjoyed by many college students, the intensive marketing of poker to college students, and campus responses to the poker phenomenon are then addressed. Finally, recommendations are presented for practice and research related to the popularity and potential problems of poker on the college campus.

A Bit About Poker and Its Popularity

The game of poker is traditionally associated with the riverboats of the nineteenth century or the dusty saloons of the Old West (see the work of McClellan and Winters earlier in this volume for a broader discussion of the history of gambling in the United States). There was a stigma attached to the game; respectable people were not ones to play it. That stigma is all but gone, and players are found everywhere. The most common form of poker played in the United States today is called Texas Hold 'Em and is the one focused on in this chapter.

In Texas Hold 'Em, each player is first dealt two cards face down, followed by a round of betting. Three community cards (called the *flop*) are then placed face up in the center of the table, followed by a second round of betting. Then the fourth and fifth community cards (called the *turn* and *river,* respectively) are placed face up on the table, each followed by a round of betting. Players use the two cards in their hand and the five community cards to make the best five-card poker hand possible. There are various forms of betting rules for Texas Hold 'Em, but the most popular and glamorized form is no-limit betting, in which a player may bet all of his chips or money at any time in a hand (called *going all in*).

Texas Hold 'Em is a relatively simple game to learn but a difficult one to master. In addition to a bit of luck, playing poker well requires skill in picking up on subtleties of human communication (called *reading tells* by poker players), reasoning, and money management. Though these are skills that many of us would be happy to see college students develop, they are a skills set that is still to be mastered for most students on our campuses. Learning them at a poker table could be an expensive lesson, in many ways.

Poker's Popularity. How popular is poker today? One need only turn on the TV and flip through the channels to get a sense of the answer. There is a strong possibility that the shows you run across on ESPN, Bravo, and the Travel Channel are high-stakes poker games, because such programs have been a rating bonanza for the networks. Watch the show go to commercial break; how many ads tout online poker locations such as Partypoker.com (which bills itself as the world's largest poker school), FullTiltPoker.com, or Pokerstars.com? Then go to the computer, browse www.thefacebook.com, and do a search to see if any poker recruits are being sought in the residence halls, fraternities, or other areas of your campus. Finally, while at the computer, use Google to perform an Internet search for "poker." As of July 22, 2005, there were 15.5 million hits for the term.

The winners of major poker tournaments are touted in the media frequently. Chris Moneymaker, a Tennessee accountant who had never played in a live tournament, entered an online tournament for a seat at the World Series of Poker and wound up taking home the top multimillion-dollar prize. The general population, including college students, can and do look at the aptly named Moneymaker and others like him and rationalize anyone can truly win big at poker.

Did you recognize Moneymaker's name before it was explained in the preceding paragraph? How about the names of Doyle Brunson, Johnny Chan, Daniel Negraneu, Phil Ivey, Annie Duke, or Kathy Liebert? They are all poker professionals who have become media celebrities. The reverse is also true. Media celebrities such as Ben Affleck, Tobey Maguire, and Meg Tilly have gained further celebrity through their poker play.

It is not just tournament winners, media-savvy poker professionals, or poker-friendly media professionals that get attention. The press seems full of mentions of college students making tens of thousands by playing poker. One example is Michael Sandberg of Princeton, who made more than $120,000 playing poker online and in the casinos of Atlantic City in a six-month period of 2004–05 (Cheng, 2005). Another is David Williams, whose story was discussed by Jim Caswell in the preceding chapter. The *Massachusetts Daily Collegian* of the University of Massachusetts describes one senior who makes $120–140 a week in earnings from poker playing with friends and another senior who plays three times a week and "has acquired the talent necessary to win enough money to get by at school without a job" (Bergeron, 2005). Faraz Jaka, a sophomore at the University of Illinois at Urbana-Champaign, notes he has made $120,000 playing poker online this past year (Needham, 2005). He stated that he plans to play professionally one day; poker is his new passion in life.

All of this attention on poker has translated to poker playing in informal settings such as bars, homes, and residence halls across the country. One indicator of the widespread nature of poker playing is that poker sets are available everywhere, from Toys R Us to supermarkets. Poker is so popular that playing card manufacturers doubled production of poker sets, and poker paraphernalia were among the top-selling December holiday gifts in 2004 (Smith, 2005). Teen playing seems to have fueled most of these sales. A card manufacturer survey revealed that on average teens play cards four times a month; 23 percent of the sample identified poker as their favorite game, and 39 percent watch poker tournaments on TV. Most states have laws expressly prohibiting teen gambling, but they are rarely enforced. Regardless of the legal issues, some parents see poker playing as a healthy recreational alternative for their children. One high school student's father plainly stated, "I would rather have my son playing poker here with his friends or at one of his friend's homes than being out drinking and driving or doing drugs" (Smith, 2005, p. 1).

Access to Poker Among College Students. If poker is so popular among college students, where are all these games taking place? Some of them are taking place in legal brick-and-mortar casinos near campuses in areas where such games are legal. It seems likely, however, that this activity makes up a modest proportion of the poker being played by students. It is reasonable to assume that a far larger proportion of the college poker playing is taking place on the Internet, in off-campus home games (which may be legal in some locales depending on the size of the bets and the age of the participants; see Chapter One), campus residence halls and Greek-letter living units, and in campus programming. Readers are referred to Stuart Brown's chapter in this volume for a detailed discussion of Internet gambling activity. This section of this chapter will focus on poker playing on campus grounds or on campus-affiliated grounds.

A quick review of campus newspapers provides evidence that poker is indeed being played on campus or campus-affiliated grounds. According to their student newspaper, most of the tournaments at Murray State University can be found in the residential colleges (Fields, 2004). One resident assistant noted that a poker game is in progress almost every night on his floor and, if the residents are not playing together, they are playing PartyPoker.com on their computers. Duke University's Wayne Manor residence hall hosts a weekly $100 buy-in game. The Wayne Manor website shows pictures of their weekly games (Duke University, 2005). A sorority at Columbia University recently held a $10 buy-in tournament, and Greeks at the University of North Carolina recently held a 175-player competition. Both games filled and had lengthy waiting lists (Cheng, 2005).

These are but a few of the stories on campus poker games that have appeared in campus publications over the past several years. They are shared simply to point out that, if students are looking to be involved in poker play on campus, they probably will not need to look far.

Marketing Poker to College Students

Student interest in poker is fueled by the steady drumbeat of marketers to get college students interested in poker. The television programs have been mentioned previously, but it goes further than that. The College Poker Championship (2004) is a prime example. It is hosted by Lou Krieger, a widely read gambling expert. Krieger states in the publicity for the tournament that "the interest in poker seems to be taking hold among college students faster than any other segment of the population" (Krieger, 2004). The tournament has students competing against one another for large scholarship awards. A person playing has to be enrolled in a college or university and must name the institution and list a student ID number as part of the registration process. There is no entry fee. Each week $500 in scholarships are awarded, $5,000 in scholarships are given in the semi-finals, and $50,000 in scholarships in the finals. Some moneys are also donated to charity. The tournament is supported by and uses the same software as royalvegaspoker.com. In fact, to play in the tournament you must download the royalvegaspoker.com software on your personal computer.

The championship has not gone unnoticed on college campuses. At the University of Illinois at Springfield, a nineteen-year-old female freshman was one of the forty-five hundred students nationwide who signed up for the tournament in 2005. She was quoted as saying, "I'm not obsessed like some of the students I see playing all the time, but I could sure use the scholarship" (United Press International, 2005).

College Poker Championship is not the only organization using tuition dollars as a lure for marketing purposes. Absolutepoker.com sponsored a win-your-tuition tournament for all university and college students in May 2005, and All N Poker, an apparel company that includes college students among its targeted client groups, sponsored a touring charity poker tournament in fraternity and sorority houses in 2004, even inviting other marketers to join them as partners in a press release (Hunt, 2004).

Casinos have also started to recruit college student poker players into their establishments, especially when situated near a college or university campus. At San Diego State University, there are several nearby Native American casinos. The Barona Casino poker room manager was quoted in the SDSU student newspaper in April 2005 as saying, "The poker industry has gotten a boom over the last few years and younger players are looking for places to play" (Shore, 2005).

Campus Responses to the Poker Craze

So what has been the response of student affairs professionals to the growing popularity of poker on the college campus? There is little in the literature to indicate any response at all. It appears most schools do not sanction or even condone gambling on campus, but there also appears to be little enforcement of those prohibitions. According to Keith Whyte, executive director of the National Council on Problem Gambling, gambling is almost omnipresent for the college population, and "administrations don't do a good job of telling students how to get help, the same way they're sending the 'prevention and responsibility' messages for alcohol, substance abuse, and date rape" (Cheng, 2005, p. 1).

Some colleges have yet to engage the issue of campus gambling (including poker play), as demonstrated in a couple of examples. At the University of Illinois (student Jaka's home campus), the dean of students office determined in 2005 that they do not permit gambling on university property (Needham, 2005). Princeton, the home campus of Michael Sandberg, has no explicit rules about gambling. They are planning on determining a policy if needed. The associate dean, who handles disciplinary issues on campus, was quoted as saying, "Were I to discover that a student was gambling online, I would probably tell them to stop and give them a warning" (Cheng, 2005, p. 1).

At Syracuse University, *The Daily Orange* reported in October 2004 that, although New York law forbids private gambling, as does the Syracuse University code of conduct, some of the residence life staff saw this as a gray issue and stated it "hasn't been on our radar" (Poster, 2004). At Boston University, a judicial affairs administrator noted, "We have not seen any trends of gambling here. There doesn't appear to be a problem at the university," and a colleague added, "It has never been brought to our attention" (Atiyeh, 2004). These quotations appeared in an article that also highlighted the many ways Boston University students gambled; the article included mention of many students playing poker and their wins and losses in online poker. At the University of Texas, Austin, the *Daily Texan* reported in a February 2004 piece that despite the Housing Department's explicit rules against poker playing students report: "Our RA says we can play cards, but we can't play for money. As long as no one acts as the casino or house (and gets a portion of the pot), it's OK and it will satisfy the players and the RA" (So, 2004).

Seventeen Virginia Tech undergraduate students were arrested in May 2005 for running an off-campus poker house. An undercover sting caused police to raid the house and seize more than $2,000 in cash and poker playing equipment. After the arrests, a Virginia Tech administrator was quoted as saying, "We are not hearing much of that (illegal gambling on campus) here. We are hearing that from colleagues around the country" (Miller and Eaton, 2005).

At other colleges, the poker craze has prompted action to limit the behavior on campus. As an example, at the University of Chicago the Resident Student Organization denied university status to a poker club, citing legal department concerns. The Housing Office is also revising the permissibility of poker in the halls (Moesel, 2004).

Still other universities have turned to poker as part of their campus programming. The Penn Poker Club at Penn State is an officially recognized student organization that receives $1,000 a semester in student fees and has regular games and tournaments on campus; sometimes the games are twice a day (Walters, 2005). One resident adviser in Elizabeth College noticed an increase of interest in the game and hosted a residential college Texas Hold 'Em tournament. The tournament was for charity from the entry fees, and the winner got a retailer gift card.

Some Iowa universities have legally sponsored intramural poker tournaments under a special license from the state (Campbell, n.d.). At Utah State, the student government hosts a Mardi Gras event every year, and the

Sigma Phi Epsilon chapter hosted a charity poker Tournament in 2005 in conjunction with the event; it attracted 120 players for a $15 buy-in (Wilson, 2005).

Implications for Practice

As Chapter Seven, by Jason Laker, on ethical considerations for institutional gambling policies, will show, student affairs administrators and others in higher education need to ask questions about current campus poker playing and gambling behavior and the appropriate support mechanisms for students who go to extremes in the activity. Are casino nights an appropriate way to do fundraising on campus? Should poker tournaments be used for intramural entertainment in campus recreation? Are poker showdowns between residence halls and within residential colleges a suitable extracurricular activity?

Student affairs professionals need to identify if there is a growing incidence of poker playing on their campus, and if so recognize the fact that this is indeed a risk-taking behavior that could have addictive qualities. The vast majority of the college-age population will try poker, play for a bit, and then abandon the activity and move on to some other pastime. However, as Chapter Six on problem and pathological gambling will demonstrate, a small percentage—5 percent or so—will become problem gamblers and have an addiction to the activity. Takushi and others (2004) highlighted the development of an integrated prevention intervention for college student gamblers. The proposal drew heavily on integrating another risk-taking behavior, alcohol prevention. The intervention combined cognitive-behavioral skills training, motivational interviewing, and personalized normative feedback, among other strategies.

Student affairs professionals should give thought to the goals and purpose of using poker as an approved programming tool on campus. It is important to plan programming more effectively in regard to gambling and poker in general. It is not a healthy assumption to have college students abstain from poker, any more than the "just say no" campaign of the 1980s solved all of the illegal drug usage problems in the United States. Some experimentation and risk taking is clearly going to occur, and this is accepted as part of the college experience. The question becomes, How much is too much, and what mixed messages are we sending?

It is left to the profession to determine to what extent we need to address the issue. Is poker simply a current fad, to be committed to the ash heap of fads such as the Pet Rock or Rubik's Cube in a few years and we should simply let it pass? Or is it something more? I believe this chapter has explored how—fad or not—the problems encountered in poker playing have the potential to be serious if not acknowledged, and the tenets of our profession demand that some attention be paid to the issue.

References

Atiyeh, C. "BU Students Take Risk on Pools, Poker." *Daily Free Press,* Apr. 2, 2004. http://www.dailyfreepress.com/global_user_elements/printpage.cfm?storyid=650084; accessed May, 17, 2005.

Bergeron, J. "Students Are Turning to Poker for Income." *Daily Collegian,* Apr. 27, 2005. http://www.dailycollegian.com/vnews/display.v?TARGET=printableandarticle_id=426f 047; accessed May 17, 2005.

Campbell, L. "Online Poker Draws Collegians." *Poker Gazette,* n.d. http://pokergazette. com/simpnews/singlenews.php?lang=enandlayout=defandcategory=1andnew; accessed May 6, 2005.

Cheng, J. "Ante Up at Dear Old Princeton: Online Poker Is a Campus Draw." *New York Times,* Mar. 14, 2005, p. A1.

College Poker Championship. "Tournament Information." *College Poker Championship.* 2004. http://www.collegepokerchampionship.com/Tournament-Information.asp?btag= CPC_Direct; accessed May 6, 2005.

Duke University. "Wayne Manor Photo Album." 2005. http://www.duke.edu/web/ waynemanor/photos.html; accessed July 22, 2005.

Fields, E. "MSU Students Join in Poker Craze." *Murray State News,* 2004. http://www. thenews.org/global_user_elements/printpage.cfm?storyid=820066; accessed May 17, 2005.

Gooley, B. "College Students Gamble with Their Education." *Poker Gazette.* (n.d.) http:// pokergazette.com/simpnews/singlenews.php?lang=enandlayout=defandcategory= 1andne; accessed May 17, 2005.

Hunt, W. "All N Poker Launches Nationwide Tour of College Campuses." *PRWEB: Press Release Newswire,* 2004. http://www.prweb.com/releases/2004/10/prweb164608.htm; accessed May 17, 2005.

Krieger, L. "The College Poker Championship, Where Cash Scholarships and Charitable Donations Are Won at the Poker Table." *Cardplayer.com.* 2004. http://www.cardplayer. com/poker_magazine/archives/printarticle.php?a_id=14058; accessed May 17, 2005.

Miller, K., and Eaton, J. "17 Tech Students Guilty in Poker Ring." *Roanoke Times,* May 6, 2005. http://www.roanoke.com/printer/printpage.aspx?arcID=23112; accessed May 17, 2005.

Moesel, A. "Dorm Gamblers Hold Their Poker Faces." *Chicago Maroon,* Feb. 20, 2004. http://maroon.uchicago.edu/news/articles/2004/02/20/dorm_gamblers_hold_t.php; accessed May 17, 2005.

Needham, C. "Student Wins $120,000 by Playing Online Poker." *Daily Illini,* May 6, 2005. http://www.dailyillini.com/global_user_elements/printpage.cfm?storyid= 949443; accessed May 17, 2005.

Poster, D. "Full House: Lucrative Prizes Draw Students to Poker Despite Illegality, Addictive Nature." *Daily Orange,* Oct. 28, 2004. http://www.dailyorange.com/global_ user_elements/printpage.cfm?storyid=784320; accessed May 17, 2005.

Shore, B. "Casinos Entice College Gamers." *Daily Aztec.* Apr. 21, 2005. http://www. thedailyaztec.com/global_user_elements/printpage.cfm?storyid=932058; accessed May 17, 2005.

Smith, K. "Hardly Child's Play: Popularity of Poker Among American Teens Raises Concerns." *Winning Streak News,* Jan. 31, 2005. http://www.winningstreak.com/blog/ archives/2005_01.php; accessed July 18, 2005.

So, Y. "Poker—Texas Style." *Daily Texan,* Feb. 19, 2004. http://www.dailytexanonline. com/global_user_elements/printpage.cfm?storyid=612197; accessed May 17, 2005.

Takushi, R. Y., Neighbors, C., Larimer, M. E., Lostutter, T. W., Cronce, J. M., and Marlatt, G. A. "Indicated Prevention of Problem Gambling Among College Students." *Journal of Gambling Studies,* 2004, *20,* 83–93.

United Press International. "4,500 College Students Vie for Poker Gold." *United Press International,* May 13, 2005. http://washtimes.com/upi-breaking/20050513=072744–3812r.htm; accessed May 17, 2005.

Walters, J. "All In." *Sports Illustrated,* Apr. 28, 2005. http://si.printthis/clickability.com/pt/cpt?action=cptandtitle=SI.com+-+SI+On+Campus+-+S; accessed May 17, 2005.

Wilson, L. "National Poker Craze Sweeps into Cache." *Hard News Café of Utah State University,* Mar. 14, 2005. http://www.hardnewscafe.usu.edu/archive/march2005/031205_poker.html; accessed May 17, 2005.

THOMAS W. HARDY *is director of housing and residence life at Valdosta State University and previously served as cochair of the Gambling Action Team at the University of Alabama.*

NEW DIRECTIONS FOR STUDENT SERVICES • DOI 10.1002/ss

4

This chapter discusses wagering on college athletics and sports wagering by college students and student athletes. Programs implemented by the NCAA and other organizations to minimize such behavior are also discussed, and recommendations for practice and research are shared.

Sports Wagering

Donald L. Rockey, Jr., Chris King

Since their inception, organized sports have been a popular target of wagering in America. College athletics are no exception, and wagering on college basketball and football has historically been very popular. As an example, Americans bet $100 million on college football alone (Davies and Abram, 2001). Concern for the integrity of college sports in light of gambling on college athletics and sports wagering on the part of college student athletes remains an issue today. Concern extends as well to sports wagering by college students at large. In fact, sports wagering has been referred to as a silent addiction affecting many college students (McCarthy, 2005).

This chapter discusses wagering on college athletics and sports wagering by college students and student athletes. The discussion begins with information regarding the scope of sports wagering, particularly wagering on college athletics. Next, sports wagering by college students is addressed. Sports wagering by student athletes is then discussed. There follow responses to the issue by legislators, college sports associations, and one student affairs professional association, and the chapter concludes with recommendations for practice and research.

Scope of Sports Wagering

One indication of the popularity of sports wagering is the sheer volume taking place. Oregon does have sports-based features as part of its lottery operations, which generate $10 million in sales; proceeds are set aside to fund

NEW DIRECTIONS FOR STUDENT SERVICES, no. 113, Spring 2006 © Wiley Periodicals, Inc.
Published online in Wiley InterScience (www.interscience.wiley.com) • DOI: 10.1002/ss.194

in-state athletic scholarships (Weinberg, 2003); Nevada is the only state with legalized sports betting in sports books. According to McCarthy (2005), $2.1 billion was wagered in 2004 at the 174 licensed sports books in the state.

Although sports books are only legal in Nevada, sports wagering through illegal sports books is still prevalent. The volume of illegal sports wagering is estimated to greatly exceed the legal (Davies and Abram, 2001), with estimates ranging from $80 to $380 billion annually (Weinberg, 2003). One way a sports bettor can place an illegal bet is via a sport bookie (an individual who takes bets and either holds them or passes them along to an illegal sports book). In the late 1990s, there were an estimated 250,000 bookies in the United States, and they did an annual business of more than $100 billion (Davies and Abram, 2001).

The Internet offers a second medium for illegal sports wagering. Although the U.S. Department of Justice holds that wagering via the Internet is illegal, sports wagering online is seen as attractive inasmuch as it offers privacy, can be accessed using credit cards, and charges lower wagering fees (known in sports wagering as the *vigorish* or *juice;* McCarthy, 2005). The amount of money bet on sports via the Internet almost doubled from $1.2 billion in 1999 to $2.17 billion in 2001 (King, 2002).

Sports Wagering and College Athletics

As mentioned earlier, college athletics, particularly football and basketball, are popular venues on which to gamble for both the college student and the general population. Of the $3 billion taken in by the legal sports books in Nevada in 2000, it was estimated that $1.2 billion was bet on college football and basketball (Davies and Abram, 2001). In fact, the National Collegiate Athletic Association (NCAA) Division I basketball tournament, which brings in more than $80 million to the legal Nevada sports books, is surpassed only by the Super Bowl, which brings in $90.8 million as the most popular sporting event on which to wager (Sessions, 2005).

History has shown that sports gambling does infiltrate college athletics in ways that threaten the integrity of the games. Davies and Abram (2001) suggested that fixing of basketball games was occurring in the 1930s, but the nation did not really take notice of the problem until the point-shaving scandal of 1951, which implicated sixty-seven student athletes and sixteen colleges, among them powerhouses such as the University of Kentucky and City College of New York. There have since been point-shaving scandals involving football or basketball at such well-respected institutions as Arizona State University, Boston College, and Northwestern University. There have also been several well-documented cases in which student athletes, and at least one coach, ran into trouble because of reported gambling activities.

Sports Wagering and College Students

Some college students attend college in Nevada, where sports wagering is legal, but the majority of college students have to rely on the illegal mediums of bookies and the Internet for sports wagering. Both are quite accessible to college students. According to Layden (1995, p. 71), it is "next to impossible to visit a college campus in search of organized gambling and not find a sophisticated on-or-off campus bookmaking operation." Bookies are commonplace on today's college campuses, but even so Internet access is ubiquitous. Once a student accesses the Internet, there are an estimated two thousand gambling sites from which to choose (Sessions, 2005). Using a credit card or other form of electronic payment, college students are finding the Internet to be an attractive medium for wagering (McClellan and others, 2001).

With such easy access to mediums for placing a sport wager, it is not surprising that sports wagering would be prevalent on college campuses. Studies of the participation rate for college students in sports wagering indicate that from one-quarter to one-half of all college students have engaged in such activity (Engwall, Hunter, and Steinberg, 2004; Knapp, Rasmussen, and Niaghi, 2003; Winters, Bengston, Dorr, and Stinchfield, 1998).

Although the research does suggest that sports wagering occurs on college campuses, it also suggests that it occurs on a much lower frequency than might be expected. Oster and Knapp (1998) found that 64 percent of UNLV students had ever gambled on sports, but the number dropped to 7 percent for those who wagered once per week or more. Similarly, LaBrie, Shaffer, LaPlante, and Wechsler (2003) reported that 8.1 percent and 10 percent of college students gambled on collegiate or professional sports, respectively, a few times during the past year, but only 0.5 percent and 0.7 percent of college students gambled on collegiate or professional sports weekly.

The findings of the research are unequivocal in finding that college males are more likely to wager on sports than females (Engwall, Hunter, and Steinberg, 2004; Knapp, Rasmussen, and Niaghi, 2003; LaBrie, Shaffer, LaPlante, and Wechsler, 2003; Oster and Knapp, 1998; Rockey, Beason, and Gilbert, 2002; Winters, Bengston, Dorr, and Stinchfield 1998). Layden (1995) found that college student sport bettors tend to be former athletes who had their career cut short, are part of a community in which to share betting tales, and have a little resourcefulness. One research study (Rockey, 2003) that compared the prevalence rate of sports wagering by fraternity members to that of nonmembers found that fraternity members had a significantly higher rate of participation in sports wagering (65.4 percent) than their nonfraternity counterparts (38.3 percent). All-male residence halls, male rodeo and sports teams, and male-dominated ROTC units are examples of campus communities that might present an opportunity to share betting tales on the college campus.

NEW DIRECTIONS FOR STUDENT SERVICES • DOI 10.1002/ss

Sports Wagering and the Student Athlete

It is clear that athletes, particularly male athletes, are among the students involved in gambling on college sports. One of the first studies (Cullen and Latessa, 1996) to measure the prevalence of student-athlete gambling on sports found that 25 percent of NCAA Division I football and basketball players wagered on college sporting events. In addition, they found that 4 percent of the student athletes surveyed wagered on games in which they played, and that 0.5 percent received money from a gambler for not playing well. Cross and Vollano (1999) surveyed 765 NCAA Division I football and basketball players and found that 45 percent of these student athletes gambled on sports. Both studies measured only sports wagering in male athletes. In a study of student athletes in the NCAA's Southeastern Conference, Rockey, Beason, and Gilbert (2002) found that overall 22.4 percent of the student athletes wagered on any sport, with 30.4 percent of males and 11.3 percent females wagering on sports. LaBrie, Shaffer, LaPlante, and Wechsler (2003) found that the prevalence rates for male and female college student athletes wagering on any sport were 33 percent and 10 percent, respectively. In addition, they found the prevalence rates dropped slightly for male and female college student athletes wagering on college sports, to 26 percent and 6 percent. According to a recent NCAA study (NCAA, 2004d), 35 percent of male student athletes and 10 percent of female student athletes engaged in sports wagering in the past year. Similar to the finding of LaBrie and colleagues (LaBrie, Shaffer, LaPlante, and Wechsler, 2003), the prevalence rates also diminished for male and female college student athletes who gambled on college sports (21 percent and 6 percent; NCAA, 2004d). Approximately 1 percent of the football players and 0.5 percent of basketball players surveyed by the NCAA (2004d) reported accepting money to play poorly. On the basis of the findings of the NCAA study and given the position of the NCAA prohibiting sports wagering by student athletes, one concludes eighty thousand NCAA student athletes per year risk their eligibility by gambling on sports.

Are student athletes more prone to problem or pathological gambling? (See Chapter Six for a definition and full discussion of these terms.) Although Rockey, Beason, and Gilbert (2002) found that student athletes had a higher prevalence rate of probable pathological (6.2 percent) and problem gambling (6.2 percent) than college nonathletes (3.3 percent and 3.4 percent), the associations were not statistically significant on the whole. The only significant association was found between female student athletes and problem gambling. According to the NCAA (2004d) study, no more than 5 percent of males and less than 0.5 percent of females within any division of the NCAA were found to be problem or pathological gamblers.

NEW DIRECTIONS FOR STUDENT SERVICES • DOI 10.1002/ss

Responses

This section of the chapter describes responses of legislators, college sports associations, and one student affairs professional association to the challenge of wagering on college athletics and wagering by students and student athletes.

Legislators. In 1992, Congress passed the Professional and Amateur Sports Protection Act, prohibiting expansion of legalized sports wagering in the United States. The law allows sports gambling to continue in its current forms in Nevada and Oregon.

Several other bills have been introduced in recent years to curb gambling on amateur and college sports. Among the recently introduced federal bills are the Amateur Sports Integrity Act (S.2340, 2000), the High School and College Gambling Prohibition Act (S. 2021, 2000), the Internet Gambling Prohibition Act (S. 474, 1997), and the Student Athlete Protection Act (H.R. 3575, 2000). Despite repeated attempts to move these pieces of legislation through Congress, to date none of them has been approved.

Sports Associations. Given the potential threat to collegiate athletics, college student athletes, and colleges and universities, it is important to review the positions of collegiate sports associations with respect to the issues addressed in this chapter.

National Collegiate Athletic Association. The NCAA opposes all forms of legal and illegal sports wagering. According to the NCAA (2004a), sports competition should be appreciated for the inherent benefits related to participation of student athletes, coaches, and institutions in fair contests, not the amount of money wagered on the outcome of the competition. With this position in mind, the NCAA adopted Bylaw 10.3, which stipulates that staff members of a member conference or athletics department and student athletes shall not knowingly provide information to individuals involved in organized gambling activities, solicit a bet, accept a bet, solicit or accept a bet on any intercollegiate competition for any item that has tangible value, or participate in any gambling activity that involves intercollegiate athletics or professional athletics (NCAA, 2004c).

Since the integrity of college athletics and protecting the student athlete from the dangers of gambling are a driving force in the NCAA, the punishment for a gambling related infraction is stiff. A student athlete who engages in sports wagering on contests involving the student athlete's institution permanently loses all remaining regular-season and postseason eligibility in all sports. If a student athlete is caught wagering on other intercollegiate sports or professional athletics, he or she becomes ineligible for regular-season and postseason competition for a minimum of one year.

In addition, the NCAA educates both student athletes and member institutions on the potential consequences of sports wagering. To help illus-

NEW DIRECTIONS FOR STUDENT SERVICES • DOI 10.1002/ss

trate the risks of gambling, former student athletes who got into trouble for gambling are instructed to talk to current student athletes (National Endowment for Financial Education and NCAA, 2004). Additional educational campaigns and resources such as "Don't Bet on It" and "Gambling With Your Life" were created to educate student athletes as well as coaches and athletic administrators on sports wagering.

Following its 2004 study of gambling behavior by college student athletes, the NCAA formed a national task force to further analyze the study's results and recommend strategies to counteract sports wagering among student athletes (NCAA, 2004b). The Task Force on Gambling focused its energy in exploring three areas: (1) awareness, education, and treatment; (2) compliance and policy; and (3) law enforcement and coalition building (NCAA, 2005b).

The task force's recommendations related to awareness, education, and treatment included several tasks to improve the understanding of the athletes and staff members. One of the tasks is to create an interactive Web site for student athletes with programming and educational materials that are division-specific and sport-specific. Another task is to offer educational programming at more NCAA events. A third task is to work with the football and golf championships staffs to develop sport-specific educational material since these sports showed a higher incidence of gambling for student athletes (NCAA, 2005a).

To address the target area of compliance and policy issues, the task force suggested a number of measures. Expanding the background checks of game officials in men's ice hockey and baseball to meet the standards that already exist in men's and women's basketball is one recommendation. Creating a list of campus best practices related to sports wagering including the educational "toolkits" is another recommendation. The final recommendation suggested reestablishing lines of communication with Las Vegas bookmakers. These legal bookmakers have been the key to discovering previous point-shaving scandals, because they are the first to recognize an uneven betting pattern on a game (Davies and Abram, 2001).

The final task force recommendation dealt with issues surrounding law enforcement and coalition building. The task force suggested developing and cultivating relationships with federal, state, and local agencies and associations. They also suggested establishing a sports wagering curriculum for all students (NCAA, 2005b).

Other Selected College Sports Associations. Neither the National Association of Intercollegiate Athletics (NAIA) nor the National Junior College Athletic Association (NJCAA) addresses as an association the issue of sports wagering by college athletes and on college athletics. According to representatives of both the NAIA and the NJCAA (personal communication with Steven Baker and Wayne Baker, Aug. 2005), the leagues do not feel regulating gambling is part of their purpose or mission. They see this is a matter best addressed at the level of individual member institutions.

Although the National Association of Student Personnel Administrators (NASPA) does not have a specific policy statement relating to wagering on college athletics or sports wagering by students and student athletes, its recommendations for practice related to the larger issue of college gambling are appropriate for use in addressing college sports wagering. NASPA recommendations for practice include reaching all students (athletes and nonathletes) through such measures as social norming education programs, treatment education programs, gambling advisory committees, and student personnel administrators' gambling education (McClellan and others, 2001).

Recommendations

In closing, student affairs professionals need to be aware that sports wagering is a popular form of entertainment for both college students and student athletes and should strive to minimize the impact of gambling through policies and programs such as those recommended by NASPA and the NCAA. Where associations see it as the responsibility of individual practitioners or member institutions to take the lead in addressing college sports wagering, it is recommended that they adopt statements explicitly stating their position and encouraging appropriate action on the part of those professionals and member institutions. It is important that student affairs professionals and professionals engaged in college student athletics work closely in developing and implementing such policies and programs. It is also important for college sports associations and student affairs professional associations to identify their common interests in addressing issues related to college sports wagering and work collaboratively in addressing those shared interests.

Despite the efforts of the NCAA and independent researchers, there is still a need for research related to wagering on college athletics and wagering by college students and student athletes. Areas in which additional research are needed are comparative studies of gambling behavior between students and student athletes, the prevalence of gambling behavior among student athletes in associations other than the NCAA, and the experiences that lead some students athletes to engage in problem and pathological gambling.

References

Amateur Sports Integrity Act, S. 2340, 2000.

Cross, M. E., and Vollano, A. G. *The Extent and Nature of Gambling Among College Student Athletes.* Ann Arbor: Athletics Department, University of Michigan, 1999.

Cullen, F. T., and Latessa, E. J. *The Extent and Sources of NCAA Rule Infractions: A National Self-Report Study of Student-Athletes.* Kansas City, Mo.: National Collegiate Athletic Association, 1996.

Davies, R. O., and Abram, R. G. *Betting the Line: Sports Wagering in American Life.* Columbus: Ohio State University Press, 2001.

Engwall, D., Hunter, R., and Steinberg, M. "Gambling and Other Risk Behaviors on University Campuses." *Journal of American College Health,* 2004, *52,* 245–255.

High School and College Gambling Prohibition Act, S. 2021, 2000.

Internet Gambling Prohibition Act, S. 474, 105th Cong., 1st Sess., 1997.

King, B. "Behind the Numbers: How U.S. Sports Dollars Are Spent Gambling." *Street and Smith Sports Business Journal,* 2002, *4,* 32–33.

Knapp, T. J., Rasmussen, C. A., and Niaghi, Z. B. "Win One for the Students: Sports Wagering by College Students." *College Student Journal,* 2003, *37,* 60–63.

LaBrie, R. A., Shaffer, H. J., LaPlante, D. A., and Wechsler, H. "Correlates of College Student Gambling in the United States." *Journal of American College Health,* 2003, *52,* 53–64.

Layden, T. "Better Education (Campus Gambling, Part 1)." *Sports Illustrated,* Apr. 3, 1995, pp. 68–90.

McCarthy, M. "Football Bettors Put Billions on the Line." *USA Today,* Sept. 8, 2005. http://www.usatoday.com/sports/football/nfl/2005–09–07-betting_x.htm?POE=click-refer; accessed Sept. 13, 2005.

McClellan, G., Caswell, J., Beck, B., Graves-Holladay, C., Mitchell, A., and Wong-O'Connor, K. *Gambling, Its Effects and Prevalence on College Campuses: Implications for Student Affairs.* Washington, D.C.: NASPA Center for Student Studies and Demographics, 2001.

National Collegiate Athletic Association. "The NCAA's Position on Sports Wagering." 2004a. http://www.ncaa.org/legislation_and_governance/eligibility_and_conduct/position_on_sports_wagering.html; accessed July 21, 2005.

National Collegiate Athletic Association. "Sports Wagering Task Force Members Focus on Education." NCAA News, Nov. 11, 2004b. http://www2.ncaa.org/media_and_events/association_news/association_updates/2004/november/1111_wagering.html; accessed July 21, 2005.

National Collegiate Athletic Association. *2004–2005 NCAA Division I Manual.* Indianapolis, Ind.: National Collegiate Athletic Association, 2004c.

National Collegiate Athletic Association. "2003 NCAA National Study on Collegiate Sports Wagering and Associated Behaviors." 2004d. http://www.ncaa.org/library/research/sports_wagering/2003/2003_sports_wagering_study.pdf; accessed Mar. 14, 2005.

National Collegiate Athletic Association. "NCAA, NABC and WBCA Partner on National 'Don't Bet on It' Campaign." *NCAA News,* Feb. 23, 2005a. http://www.ncaa.org/media_and_events/press_room/2005/february/20050223_dontbetonitreleasebkb.html; accessed July 21, 2005.

National Collegiate Athletic Association. "NCAA Task Force Recommends More Education, Partnering with Other Groups to Decrease Gambling on Sports." *NCAA News,* July 19, 2005b. http://www.ncaa.org/media_and_events/press_room/2005/july/20050719_d1_manco_rls.html; accessed July 21, 2005.

National Endowment for Financial Education and NCAA. *Don't Bet on It.* www.ncaa.org/gambling/dontbetonit/2004.pdf; accessed Dec. 28, 2005.

Oster, S., and Knapp, T. "Sports Betting by College Students: Who Bets and How Often?" *College Student Journal,* 1998, *32,* 289–292.

Professional and Amateur Sports Protection Act, 28 U.S.C. § 3701, 1992.

Rockey, D., Beason, K., and Gilbert, J. "Gambling by College Athletes: An Association Between Problem Gambling and Athletes." *Electronic Journal of Gambling Issues,* 2002, vol. 7. http://www.camh.net/egambling/issue7/research/college_gambling.html; accessed July 11, 2005.

Rockey, D. L. "Association Between Problem Gambling in Student-Athletes and Non-Athletes and Greek and Non-Greek Affiliated Students." Paper presented at National Conference on Problem Gambling, sponsored by National Council on Problem Gambling, Louisville, Ky., June 19–21, 2003.

Sessions, D. "Rise in Gambling Troubles NCAA." *Duluth News Tribune*, Mar., 15, 2005. http://www.responsiblegambling.org/articles/Rise_in_gambling_troubles_NCAA_march_ madness_college.pdf; accessed July 12, 2005.

Student Athlete Protection Act, H.R. 3575, 2000.

Weinberg, A. "The Case for Legal Sports Gambling." *Forbes*, Jan. 27, 2003. http://www.forbes.com/2003/01/27/cx_aw_0127gambling.html; accessed Oct. 9, 2005.

Winters, K. C., Bengston, P., Dorr, D., and Stinchfield, R. "Prevalence and Risk Factors of Problem Gambling Among College Students." *Psychology of Addictive Behaviors*, 1998, *12*, 127–135.

DONALD L. ROCKEY, JR., *is assistant professor of recreation and sport management in the Department of Health, Physical Education, and Recreation at Coastal Carolina University.*

CHRIS KING *is associate athletics director of compliance at the University of Alabama.*

This chapter focuses on the issues surrounding the growth of online gambling on college and university campuses.

The Surge in Online Gambling on College Campuses

Stuart J. Brown

The Internet's penetration into American society is widespread and ubiquitous. According to a March 2005 survey by the Pew Internet and American Life Project, 67 percent of individuals eighteen or older—136 million adults—use the Internet. When usage is limited to the eighteen-to-twenty-nine-year-old age group, the bracket that includes most college and university students, the percentage skyrockets to 84 percent (Rainie and Horrigan, 2005).

One of the online activities that have seen a phenomenal growth rate among undergraduates at institutions of higher education is online gambling ("Online Gambling Growing Rapidly," 1999). In fact, college and university students are reportedly the fastest growing sector of online gamblers (Zewe, 1998).

Gambling sites are inviting, whether emulating the glitz and flashing lights of a bricks-and-mortar casino or matter-of-factly outlining the numerous playing options for the multitude of browsers. These Web sites are exceptionally user-friendly, allowing quick downloading of, for example, free poker playing software. Students have a variety of payment options available to them to nourish their gambling activities: credit cards, debit cards, personal checks, and wire transfers (Kanne and others, 2002).

This chapter briefly looks at college gambling and discusses the upsurge of online gambling by college and university students, the reasons for the upsurge in this activity, and the problems associated with this type of involvement. Concluding the chapter are recommendations practitioners can use on their campus.

NEW DIRECTIONS FOR STUDENT SERVICES, no. 113, Spring 2006 © Wiley Periodicals, Inc.
Published online in Wiley InterScience (www.interscience.wiley.com) • DOI: 10.1002/ss.195

Online Gambling Gains in Popularity

The growth of online gambling, which could be broadly be defined as gambling that occurs through use of the Internet, is a recent phenomenon. Whereas in the mid-1990s there were fewer than twenty-five online gambling sites on the Internet ("Financial Aspects of Internet gaming . . . ," 2001) today there are more than two thousand (Nguyen, 2005). Typing *online poker* (see Hardy's discussion in Chapter Three for further discussion of the current poker craze) or *online casino* in any of the popular Web search engines produces millions of identified links to actual online gambling sites, instructional Web pages, and articles on the subject.

The online casinos tout blackjack, craps, roulette, poker, slot machines, and more. The Intercasino.com site, one of the most frequented Internet casinos, "offers a version of nearly every game you can find on a casino floor, from slots and video poker to multiplayer games such as blackjack and baccarat" (Appelbaum, 2005).

For individuals seeking to branch out beyond the realm of online casinos, there are sites such as www.sportsbook.com, which is "one of the world's busiest sports book" Web sites (Appelbaum, 2005). Almost any type of wager is available on its pages, including the National Football League, Major League Baseball, golf, NASCAR, horse racing, and the Superbowl.

The Web site PokerPulse.com, which bills itself as "the recognized leader in providing accurate, actionable information to the online multiplayer poker industry and to the online player community," ranks online poker sites "based on observed total real money ring game and tournament players." Web sites with such names as PartyPoker, PokerStars, and PokerRoom. com topped the PokerPulse.com chart in July 2005. As of May 2005, according to its statistics, there were more than 1.8 million "active real money players online wagering $200 million each day" (PokerPulse.com, 2005). In an April 2005 article for the *Detroit News,* reporter Joel J. Smith reported that "during peak hours on EmpirePoker.com, nearly 70,000 people worldwide simultaneously play poker at 8,000 poker tables. Stakes can range from a few dollars up to $1 million" (Smith, 2005).

This year's College Poker Championship, an online tournament with free registration for all college and university undergraduates, attracted twenty-five thousand students from fifty-five countries (Krieger, 2005). The figure represented a tenfold increase over the previous year. The winner, who took home a $41,000 academic scholarship, was Chad Flood, a twenty-year-old junior from the University of Minnesota-Twin Cities.

Estimates of the online gambling profits for 2005 are in the $10 billion range, a 40 percent increase over the previous year (Walters, 2005). An increase to $14.5 billion for 2006 has been projected by the U.S. Government Accountability Office (Groover, 2005). The initial public offering for PartyGaming on the London Exchange was a hot commodity, valuing the company at more than $9 billion. This makes it more valuable than Harrah's Entertainment and almost as valuable as MGM Mirage (Timmons and Pfanner, 2005), two of the largest operators of bricks-and-mortar casino hotels in the world.

Reasons for Increase in Online Gambling

Even though there are a number of unresolved issues surrounding online gambling, enthusiasm for online gambling—particularly among college students—continues to grow. The popularity in online gambling can be attributed to several causes.

Popular Media. There are several television series set in Las Vegas and focusing on various aspects of gambling life and culture. Poker tournaments are regularly scheduled broadcasts on such cable channels as Bravo, ESPN, and the Travel Channel. They come complete with strategically placed cameras and color commentators hyping the action. The Spike television network has a weekly Casino Cinema night that mixes poker playing advice and demonstrations during commercial breaks of the broadcast movie. The recently concluded 2005 Poker World Series attracted front-page coverage from such stalwarts of journalism as the *New York Times* and the *Los Angeles Times*. In fact, "poker is now the third most watched televised sport on cable TV, trailing only auto racing and football" (Emling, 2005).

Comfort Level with Technology. The GenNet students, college and university undergraduates, "have grown up with the Internet, cell phones, and other fruits of the IT revolution" (Ward, 2005). They have been accessing the Internet since grade school, and their use of Web-based applications is second-nature to them (Kanne and others, 2002). According to a July 2005 report from the Pew Internet and American Life Project, "87 percent of those aged 12 to 17 now use the Internet" (Lenhart, Madden, and Hitlin, 2005). This familiarity with technology has made use of online gambling an effortless exercise.

Twenty-Four, Seven Access. Most institutions of higher education tout free, universal high-speed connections on their campus. The hardwire access is usually available in residence hall rooms, common areas, and the library. More often than not, wireless connections are spreading across all corners of a campus. These hookups make student access to online gambling sites as effortless as the click of a mouse—no matter the day or time (Walters, 2005).

Anonymity. No one knows who you are, where you are playing, or your age in an online gambling site. Players are viewed only as screen names or on-screen icons. If you make an ill-advised move or dumb mistake, you are protected by the anonymity of cyberspace (Walters, 2005).

Access to Credit. Today's undergraduate is most likely equipped with at least one credit card. Bill Saum, former director of agent gambling and amateurism activities of the National Collegiate Athletic Association, reported that "a study by Nellie Mae indicates that 78 percent of college students have credit cards. Thirty-two percent have four or more" ("Financial Aspects of Internet Gaming . . . ," 2001). Kevin Whyte, executive director of the National Council on Problem Gambling, stated that having college and university students armed with credit cards "is going to result in a lot more internet gambling among adolescents" ("Financial Aspects of Internet Gaming . . . ," 2001).

Learning the Ropes. Most online gambling Web sites entice participants with a play money option. Individuals can learn various poker games and practice at single-table or multitable tournaments without spending a dime. As SI.com reporter John Walters states, "you can play 150 hands an hour in one game, easily, online. In poker, as with so many endeavors in life, experience is the best teacher" (Walters, 2005).

Blogs. Online journals have grown from "an estimated 4.8 million [in December 2004] . . . up from just 100,000 two years ago" ("The Business of Blogging," 2004). Online gambling blogs play into the narcissism in today's society, where students think their views will be absorbed by others (personal correspondence with M. Kahn, 2005).

Although Internet gambling has proliferated, it has done so mired in controversy. First and foremost is the questionable legality of online gambling. Citing the Interstate Wire Act of 1961, the federal government has banned online gambling by companies headquartered on U.S. soil. It is for this reason that all online gambling sites are offshore, in such locales as the Caribbean, Antigua, Belize, and Gibraltar (Appelbaum, 2005; Walters, 2005; Weir, 2003). There they can lure players from the United States without concern of prosecution by American authorities. Second, there are few, if any, regulations for the way these offshore companies operate. The lack of regulation has inhibited some gamblers from being involved in Internet wagering. Great Britain has stepped into this void. Looking to cash in on a powerful new revenue stream, the United Kingdom legalized online gambling in spring 2005 and set up a commission to oversee its practices (Timmons and Pfanner, 2005). Third, without the ability to "see" the patron, assessing the age of online gamblers is next to impossible. Virtual identification cards have not been developed, so tech-savvy, underage individuals can easily circumvent verification systems implemented on Web sites ("Kids Can Log on . . . ," 2005; Weir, 2003). Lastly, online gambling sites have had "either hard-to-find warnings about underage gambling, inadequate warnings or none at all" ("FTC Warns Consumers . . . ," 2002).

Problems Related to Online Gambling

Given what is known about college student gambling behavior, it is reasonable to assume that the effects of the upsurge in online gambling are magnified on college campuses. Researchers have found that college and

NEW DIRECTIONS FOR STUDENT SERVICES • DOI 10.1002/ss

university students had a much higher rate of gambling problems than the general adult population (Messerlian, 2004; Neighbors, Lostutter, Cronce, and Larimer, 2002; Shaffer and others, 2005; Shaffer, Hall, and Vander Bilt, 1999). Ed Looney, director of the New Jersey Council on Compulsive Gambling, says "the No. 1 form of problem gambling for college students is Internet betting on sports" (Weir, 2003). Blogger Lauren Patrizi, a self-professed gambler and student at Loyola University Chicago, characterizes online gambling as the current drug of choice on campus (Patrizi, 2005).

One area in which there is currently a great deal of activity regarding the intersecting jurisdictions of state and federal authority over gambling is Internet gambling (Manter, 2003; Parke and Griffiths, 2004). The jurisdictional waters in this area have been even further muddied by the entrance of global governing agencies into the dispute (CongressDaily.com, 2005). This is an area of the law that ought to be of particular interest to college and university communities in the United States, given the number of students engaging in Internet gambling, the extensive Internet access available to students via institutional resources, and the federal government's assertion that the simple act of allowing advertising for Internet gambling to appear in print or broadcast format may be abetting criminal activity (U.S. Department of Justice, 2003).

Recommendations

Campus administrators need to recognize that online gambling is a problem that must be addressed, both at the policy level and through prevention and education efforts. Institutions have been criticized for accomplishing too little in their efforts to confront the online gambling issue (Kanne and others, 2002; Shaffer and others, 2005; Shaffer, Forman, Scanlan, and Smith, 2000; Sharma, 2004). Most of the time and energy of administrators has gone into substance abuse programs and prevention. "Colleges, already struggling to reduce underage drinking, drug use, and even online music piracy, are stretched too thin to allocate resources to combat this seemingly less sinister problem" (Sharma, 2004, p. 1). Researchers have lamented that institutions are missing a golden opportunity to work with students during their academic career (Shaffer and others, 2005). Tom Tucker, director of the California Council on Problem Gambling, says that "students are doomed to be the next generation of problem gamblers without prevention education at the college level" (Kanne and others, 2002).

Recommendations for Practitioners. Many of the recommendations described here could be quickly instituted at colleges or universities. Most of these proposals could be attached to existing training programs, for example, within the Office of Residence Life. In additional, there are some basic program and policy reviews that can be done on campus:

- *Introduce the problems associated with online gambling at new student orientation.* For example, a current undergraduate who has had issues with online gambling could speak to the incoming undergraduates. Afterward, departments that provide assistance to students—counseling, mental health, and so on—could talk about awareness, warning signs, and where students can go for support if needed.
- *Involve staff.* Include information sessions for student and professional staff at training programs for department personnel who work with students who might have gambling problems and addiction. The information should include easy-to-understand reference material, campus phone numbers to call, and general readings on the subject.
- *Hold workshops on campus.* College officials, from the Office of Student Affairs or Health Services or Counseling Services, should hold on-campus workshops on the online gambling problems and addiction. On a residential campus, these programs should be held primarily, but not totally, in conjunction with the Office of Residence Life. They can be incorporated into the educational programming component for residence halls. On a commuter campus, the workshops need to be offered at a time advantageous to the student body, whether during traditional office hours or afterwards.
- *Review institutional conduct codes.* Ensure they adequately address online gambling issues. Once changes or additions have been implemented, they should be adequately publicized to the student body. The information could be disseminated through campus workshops, an announcement and links on the school Web site, press releases, and stories in the campus press and local publications.
- *Publish policies in student handbooks.* Have information about institutional policies toward online gambling clearly outlined in the student handbook and the student code of conduct. The information should be easily located on the school Web site with links from such offices as the Dean of Students, Health Services, Counseling, and so forth pointing back to this page.
- *Use parent orientation programs.* Since parents are sometimes the first to discover a problem by way of their credit card statement, information on online gambling should be presented at parent orientation programs. Again, a current student who had an online gambling problem could speak to the assembled parents. Officials from departments that assist undergraduates with online gambling problems and addictions could also speak. Frequent bulletins should be included in parent newsletters or parent-oriented Web pages.
- *Make use of counseling service professionals.* Have counseling services or mental health professionals keep the administration apprised of the online gambling problem on campus. They are probably the most appropriate office(s) to monitor the pulse of the campus since they may be the first to become aware of problems at the institution.

NEW DIRECTIONS FOR STUDENT SERVICES • DOI 10.1002/ss

• *Curtail campus sponsored casino nights and poker tournaments at the school.* Officially sanctioned activities such as these could send a mixed message to students: gambling is not allowed on campus, but the activity is fine as long as it is condoned by the administration. Yet since unsanctioned gambling does take place—especially in the residence halls—having information about gambling addiction present throughout the campus would be a proactive step.

Further Research Considerations. The field of online gambling research is new and fluid. It changes and evolves with the latest technological twist. Therefore, investigation into the effect of online gambling on the campus population needs to continue. In addition to the recommendations for practice, here are recommendations for additional research needed at the nexus between online gambling and campus communities:

• Does online gambling promote other unhealthy behaviors such as alcoholism and drug abuse? Is there a correlation between online gambling and other addictions? Research into these questions can assist mental health practitioners and counselors to more readily identify problems on campus.

• How successful, academically, are students who participate in online gambling? Are grades unaffected? Do undergraduates identified as having a problem with online gambling have a lower grade point average? Research into these questions may signify more academic intervention programs as a way to address online gambling issues.

• What is the effect of online gambling on the socialization process at a school, whether in a residence hall or the campus at large? Do students feel compelled to gamble as a way of fitting in to the campus milieu? Are students involved in online gambling because of real or perceived lack of co-curricular activities on campus?

• How is community development affected within the confines of a residential facility? Do undergraduates spend more time on their computers gambling than socializing within the residence hall? Conversely, has online gambling activity promoted interaction among the residential population?

• Is online gambling a real issue on college and university campuses, or is it the latest Web-based problem being exploited by the media? Should colleges and universities be expending resources to address online gambling, or are there more pressing problems to be concerned with?

Conclusion

Is online gambling the addiction of the new millennium for college and university students? Current research and anecdotal evidence would point in this direction, but much more research needs to be done to accurately gauge the depth of the situation. Technologically savvy students, exposed to the

Internet at such an early age, have seemingly gravitated to online casinos and poker Web sites. The evidence, witnessed with fascination by all types of media outlets, the reported increase in the number of students partaking in this outlet, and the increased concerns on the part of campus administrators point to a problem that needs to be addressed and further examined.

References

Appelbaum, B. "It's Easy; It's Quick; It's Online." *Knight Ridder Tribune Business,* May 2005, p. 1.

"The Business of Blogging." *Business Week,* Dec. 13, 2004. http://www.businessweek. com/magazine/content/04_50/b3912115_mz016.htm; accessed Aug. 24, 2005.

CongressDaily.com. "WTO Says Online Gambling Ban Needs Changes." Apr. 7, 2005. http://nationaljournal.com/about/congressdaily; accessed July 10, 2005.

Emling, S. "Online Gambling Hits Growing Jackpot; Illegality Doesn't Stem Popularity." *Atlanta Journal Constitution,* Aug. 28, 2005, p. 3F.

"FTC Warns Consumers About Online Gambling and Children." Federal Trade Commission, 2002. http://www.ftc.gov/opa/2002/06/onlinegambling.htm; accessed June 30, 2005.

"Financial Aspects of Internet Gaming: Good Gamble or Bad Bet?" July 12, 2001. U.S. House of Representatives, Subcommittee on Oversight and Investigations, Committee on Financial Services. http://commdocs.house.gov/committees/bank/hba74100.000/ hba74100_0.HTM; accessed July 24, 2005.

Groover, J. "States Bet on Online Gambling Revenues." *American City and County,* May 2005, pp. 16–18.

Interstate Wire Act, 18 USC sec. 1084 (1961).

Kanne, J., Dunch, D., Tone, J., Schellinger, N., Bechen, E., Allrich, H., Moon, J., McCarthy, S., Vidunas, L., Calderon, N., and Tieu, A. "You're So Money." *Metro,* Feb. 7–14, 2002. http://www.metroactive.com/papers/metro/02.07.02/gambling1–0206. html; accessed July 24, 2005.

"Kids Can Log on and Lose Thousands with No Safeguards or Protections." (Press release). Sen. Charles E. Schumer, New York, Mar. 20, 2005. http://schumer.senate. gov/SchumerWebsite/pressroom/press_releases/2005/PR41537.Online percent20Gambling.032005.html; accessed July 24, 2005.

Krieger, L. "2005 College Poker Championship." 2005. http://www.pokermagazine. com/Poker-Tournaments/poker_news_college_tournament.html; accessed June 28, 2005.

Lenhart, A., Madden, M., and Hitlin, P. "Teens and Technology: Youth Are Leading the Transition to a Fully Wired and Mobile Nation." Pew Internet and American Life Project, July 27, 2005, pp. 1–56.

Manter, G. "The Pending Determination of the Legality of Internet Gambling in the United States." *Duke Law and Technology Review,* 2003. http://www.law.duke.edu/jour-nals/dltr/articles/2003dltr0016.html; accessed July 21, 2005.

Messerlian, C. "Early Identification of At-Risk Gamblers." *Youth Gambling International,* 2004, *4,* 9.

Neighbors, C., Lostutter, T. W., Cronce, J. M., and Larimer, M. E. "Exploring College Student Gambling Motivation." *Journal of Gambling Studies,* 2002, *18,* 361–370.

Nguyen, M. "Hold 'Em at the Click of a Mouse." *Daily Aztec,* Apr. 21, 2005. http://aztec. collegepublisher.com/media/paper741/news/2005/04/21/City/Hold-em.At. The.Click.Of.A.Mouse-932084.shtml; accessed July 24, 2005.

"Online Gambling Growing Rapidly." 1999. *Gambling Magazine.* http://www.gambling-magazine.com/articles/37/37–105.htm; accessed July 20, 2005.

Parke, A., and Griffiths, M. "Why Internet Gambling Prohibition Will Ultimately Fail." *Gaming Law Review,* 2004, *8,* 295–299.

Patrizi, L. "The New Drug on College Campuses." 2005. http://www.campusprogress.org/page/community/post/laurenpatrizi/Bjf; accessed July 20, 2005.

PokerPulse.com. 2005. http://www.pokerpulse.com; accessed July 24, 2005.

Rainie, L., and Horrigan, J. *A Decade of Adoption: How the Internet Has Woven Itself into American Life.* Pew Internet and American Life Project, 2005. http://www.pewinternet.org/pdfs/Internet_Status_2005.pdf; accessed July 24, 2005.

Shaffer, H., Donato, A., LaBrie, R., Kidman, R., and LaPlante, D. "The Epidemiology of College Alcohol and Gambling Policies." *Harm Reduction Journal,* 2005, *2,* 1–20.

Shaffer, H. J., Forman, D. P., Scanlan, K. M., and Smith, F. "Awareness of Gambling Related Problems, Policies and Educational Programs Among High School and College Administrators." *Journal of Gambling Studies,* 2000, *16*(1), 93–101.

Shaffer, H., Hall, M., and Vander Bilt, J. "Estimating the Prevalence of Disordered Gambling Behavior in the United States and Canada: A Research Synthesis." *American Journal of Public Health,* 1999, *89,* 1369–1376.

Sharma, S. "Student Gambling." *BT Magazine,* Fall 2004. http://www.businesstoday.org/magazine/issues/1/9.php; accessed July 20, 2005.

Smith, J. "Online Poker Flush with New Players." *Detnews.com,* Apr. 10, 2005. http://www.detnews.com/2005/casinonews/0504/22/B01–145429.htm; accessed July 24, 2005.

Timmons, H., and Pfanner, E. "Online Gambling Shares Climb 11% in Debut Day." *New York Times,* June 28, 2005, p. C6.

U.S. Department of Justice. "Advertising for Internet Gambling and Offshore Sports-book Operations." June 11, 2003. http://www.igamingnews.com/articles/files/NAB_letter-030611.pdf; accessed July 18, 2005.

Walters, J. "Computer Friendly: Gambling Has Found a Growing Fan Base Online." *SI.com,* May 24, 2005. http://sportsillustrated.cnn.com/2005/more/05/23/internet.poker/index.html; retrieved July 10, 2005.

Ward, D. "Make Room for Generation Net: A Cultural Imperative." *Defense AT and L,* 2005, *56.* http://find.galegroup.com/itx/infomark.do?andtype=retrieveandtabID=T002andprodId=ITOFanddocId=A132839889andsource=galeandsrcprod=ITOFanduser GroupName=2251andversion=1.0; accessed Sept. 10, 2005.

Weir, T. "Online Sports Betting Spins out of Control." *USA Today,* Aug. 22, 2003. http://www.usatoday.com/sports/2003–08–21-online-betting_x.htm; accessed July 20, 2005.

Zewe, C. "Should Online Gambling Be Regulated?" *Cable News Network,* Mar. 12, 1998. http://www.cnn.com/TECH/computing/9803/12/internet.gambling/; accessed July 24, 2005.

STUART J. BROWN *is assistant dean of students at the University of Connecticut, Waterbury, campus and president of StudentAffairs.com.*

6

This chapter examines problem and pathological gambling among college students and reports on prevalence rate, risk and protective factors, prevention and intervention, and recommendations for college student personnel and other university administrators.

Problem and Pathological Gambling Among College Students

Randy Stinchfield, William E. Hanson, Douglas H. Olson

College students exhibit a continuum of gambling behavior, from none to experimenting with gambling, to regular gambling, to excessive gambling with concomitant adverse consequences. Many college students gamble. Most do not experience adverse consequences, but there are a small percentage who become problem gamblers (Winters, Bengston, Dorr, and Stinchfield, 1998).

Many youths begin gambling at an early age, even earlier than they begin other risky behaviors such as tobacco and alcohol use (Ladouceur, Dube, and Bujold, 1994a; Stinchfield, 2004). A longitudinal study that followed an adolescent sample into young adulthood found that rates of gambling and problem gambling remained fairly stable over time; however, there was a shift away from informal games to legalized games as youths came of legal age (Winters, Stinchfield, and Kim, 1995). Some young men and women recently arrived at college have begun participating in legalized gambling, a new "rite of passage" for many young adults, while others will go through this rite for the first time in college. Still other students have been gambling for years informally through betting on games of personal skill, cards, and sporting events.

This chapter, which is divided into five sections, presents information related to problem and pathological gambling by college students. In the first section, we present an overview of problem and pathological gambling, including definitions, prevalence rates, and signs and symptoms. In the sec-

NEW DIRECTIONS FOR STUDENT SERVICES, no. 113, Spring 2006 © Wiley Periodicals, Inc.
Published online in Wiley InterScience (www.interscience.wiley.com) • DOI: 10.1002/ss.196

ond section, we discuss risk and protective factors associated with college student gambling. In the third section, we briefly describe problem gambling screening and assessment instruments. In the fourth section, we highlight existing prevention and intervention approaches that are geared toward college students. Finally, we conclude by offering recommendations for future research on this important, yet generally understudied, topic.

Problem and Pathological Gambling

Problem gambling is not defined by how often someone gambles or how much money the person loses. Rather, it is defined by whether or not the individual's life is disrupted by the gambling—namely, if gambling takes precedence over other activities and the individual experiences adverse consequences because of gambling. For a college student, adverse consequences may include loss of money that was intended for tuition or room and board, missing classes thanks to gambling, sleep deprivation caused by gambling through the night at a casino or online, and failing grades, to name a few. Though many labels and terms have been bantered about, the most commonly used terms are *problem gambling* and *pathological gambling*. Problem gambling is a general term referring to all individuals who have any problems associated with their gambling, including those who are diagnosed as pathological gamblers.

In contrast, pathological gambling (PG) is a psychiatric diagnosis, limited to only those individuals who satisfy the diagnostic criteria described in the *Diagnostic and Statistical Manual of Mental Disorders–Fourth Edition* (DSM-IV; American Psychiatric Association, 1994). PG was first identified as a mental disorder by the APA in 1980 and is defined as a persistent and recurrent maladaptive gambling behavior that disrupts personal, family, or vocational pursuits (American Psychiatric Association, 1994). The three cardinal signs of PG are (1) preoccupation with gambling and obtaining money with which to gamble; (2) loss of control of one's gambling, that is, not following reasonable limits of time and money spent on gambling; and (3) continuation of gambling despite adverse consequences, such as continuing to gamble in spite of losing large sums of money. The diagnostic criteria for PG are similar to those of substance use disorders and share a number of signs and symptoms, such as tolerance and withdrawal.

How many college students are problem gamblers? A number of surveys have yielded the prevalence rate of problem gambling among college samples (Shaffer, Hall, and Vander Bilt, 1997). Lesieur and others (1991) administered the South Oaks Gambling Screen (SOGS) to 1,771 students on multiple campuses across New York, New Jersey, Nevada, Oklahoma, and Texas. They found that 9.3 percent of the men and 2.4 percent of the women scored in the probable pathological gambling (PPG) range. Winters, Bengston, Dorr, and Stinchfield (1998) administered the SOGS to 1,361 students on two college campuses in Minnesota and found that 4.9 percent of men and 1.0 percent of women scored in the PPG range. Engwall, Hunter, and Steinberg (2004) gave a modified version of the SOGS to 1,350 students on four campuses of Connecticut State University during the fall of 2000 and found that 8.5 percent of the men and 1.9 percent of the women scored in the PPG range. Ladouceur, Dube, and Bujold (1994b) used the SOGS with 1,471 students at three colleges in Quebec and found 5.7 percent of the men and 0.6 percent of the women scoring in the PPG range. If we summarize these four studies, we find that approximately 5–9 percent of men and 1–2 percent of women are PPG on college campuses in North America.

Risk and Protective Factors Associated with College Student Gambling

Although much has been written about "correlates," or factors, associated with problem gambling among the general public, relatively little has been written about factors associated with college student gambling (LaBrie, Shaffer, LaPlante, and Wechsler, 2003; Lesieur and others, 1991; Stinchfield and Winters, 2004; Winters, Bengston, Dorr, and Stinchfield, 1998). However, in a recent large-scale, nationwide survey of 10,765 college students, LaBrie, Shaffer, LaPlante, and Wechsler (2003) identified twenty-seven factors that ". . . were significantly associated with the decision to gamble . . ." (p. 58). Rather than discuss each of these factors individually, we highlight the most salient ones, including prominent risk factors such as substance abuse and dependence, gender, and ethnicity. We will highlight, to the extent possible, salient protective factors.

Out of all possible risk factors, one of the most salient is substance use, abuse, and dependence. The link between alcohol, illicit drug, and tobacco use and gambling and problem gambling is strong, having been firmly established in the empirical literature (Clark, 2003; Engwall, Hunter, and Steinberg, 2004; Giacopassi, Stitt, and Vandiver, 1998; LaBrie Shaffer, LaPlante, and Wechsler, 2003; Ladouceur, Dube, and Bujold, 1994b; Welte and others, 2004; Winters, Bengston, Dorr, and Stinchfield, 1998). In the majority of studies conducted on this topic, heavy alcohol use was highly predictive of problem gambling. In one study, for example, it was associated with the size of bets made while gambling, unanticipated withdrawal of extra money at the casino, and loss of more money than could be reasonably afforded (Giacopassi, Stitt, and Vandiver, 1998). Thus, the gambling-substance relationship, though not necessarily causal in nature, appears to be robust, especially for men.

In terms of gender, males are more involved in gambling than females (Kweitel and Allen, 1998; LaBrie, Shaffer, LaPlante, and Wechsler, 2003; Platz, Knapp, and Crossman, 2005; Stinchfield, 2000; Welte and others, 2004; Winters, Bengston, Dorr, and Stinchfield, 1998), and males also have a higher rate of problem gambling than females (Ladouceur, Dube, and Bujold, 1994b; Lesieur and others, 1991; Shaffer, Hall, and Vander Bilt, 1997; Winters, Bengston, Dorr, and Stinchfield, 1998). Consequently, gender is another salient risk factor. It is unclear, though, whether the observed gender differences relate to male-female differences in other areas—for example, general motivation to gamble (Neighbors and Larimer, 2004; Neighbors, Lostutter, Cronce, and Larimer, 2002), issues of perceived control (Baboushkin, Hardoon, Derevensky, and Gupta, 2001)—or to personality and cognitive variables such as impulsivity, sensation seeking, and risk taking (Breen and Zuckerman, 1999; Langewisch and Frisch, 1998).

Ethnicity, like gender, is yet another salient risk factor. Studies have shown that individuals who are ethnically diverse (for example, African American, Asian American) tend to gamble more often than their European American counterparts (Lesieur and others, 1991; Stinchfield, 2000; Welte and others, 2004). In fact, Welte and colleagues (2004) concluded, in their nationally representative survey study of adults, that ". . . being African American, Hispanic, or Asian and having low SES are significant risk factors for pathological gambling, even after taking into account gambling frequency, size of wins and losses, number of types of gambling, substance use, and criminal offending" (p. 332). Far too few studies have been conducted, however, on this factor to make any definitive conclusions.

The explanatory value of ethnicity and for that matter gender as mediating variables is, at best, limited, and at worst more-or-less unknown. Knowing that a college student is, for example, an African American male tells you little if anything about the extent of problem gambling risk that the student actually experiences. It is more important, therefore, to pay attention to other known risk factors, such as a student's overall level of gambling activity, or "volume," general gambling versatility (pull tabs *and* casinos; Welte and others, 2004), tendency to minimize losses (Baboushkin, Hardoon, Derevensky, and Gupta, 2001), general academic performance (LaBrie, Shaffer, LaPlante, and Wechsler, 2003; Winters, Bengston, Dorr, and Stinchfield, 1998), and typical leisure or extracurricular activities (time spent watching television, participation in athletics; LaBrie, Shaffer, LaPlante, and Wechsler, 2003). It is also important to pay attention to parental or guardian history of gambling (Lesieur and others, 1991; Winters, Bengston, Dorr, and Stinchfield, 1998). As noted by Winters and colleagues (1998), ". . . the relative risk of problem gambling is about three to five times greater when the family history is positive . . . " (p. 133).

Although the research presented thus far has focused on risk factors, we want to mention two known protective factors: one's belief that the arts and religion are important, and having a parent who has a college degree (LaBrie, Shaffer, LaPlante, and Wechsler, 2003). More research is clearly needed on factors of this type, factors that may help protect or buffer college students from the negative consequences of problem gambling.

Being familiar with risk and protective factors is an important first step in early recognition of college students who may be gambling excessively. However, to distinguish reliably between those students who gamble for fun, with no attendant problems, and those who gamble pathologically, one also needs to be familiar with more formal, psychometrically sound screening and assessment instruments, a few of which are discussed in the next section.

Problem and Pathological Gambling Screening and Assessment Instruments

College student counseling services need to be able to screen for problem gambling in order to plan for and provide appropriate referral and treatment services (Lesieur and others, 1991). Most problem gambling instruments are relatively new and have not received rigorous psychometric evaluation (National Research Council, 1999). There is also a paucity of research on the measurement of problem gambling among special populations in general, and college students in particular. In most research on problem gambling among college students, existing instruments designed for adults have been used. Most of these instruments assess some or all of the diagnostic criteria listed in the DSM-IV (APA, 1994). Two instruments are briefly described here; for a more thorough description of gambling assessment instruments, see Stinchfield, Govoni, and Frisch (2004).

The most commonly used instrument to assess problem gambling is the South Oaks Gambling Screen (SOGS), developed by Lesieur and Blume (1987). The SOGS has extensive testing of its reliability, validity, and classification accuracy (Lesieur and Blume, 1987; Stinchfield, 2002). The twenty-item SOGS is scored by summing the number of items endorsed; a cut score of 5 or more indicates PPG. The content of the SOGS includes items that inquire about spending more time or money gambling than intended, hiding evidence of one's gambling, arguing with family members about one's gambling, and borrowing money from a variety of sources to gamble or pay gambling debts.

The Gambling Behavior Interview (GBI) is a seventy-six-item instrument designed to measure signs and symptoms of problem gambling (Stinchfield, 2002, 2003; Stinchfield, Govoni, and Frisch, 2005). The GBI has a past-twelve-months time frame and may be administered in approximately fifteen minutes, or a much shorter time if the respondent has not gambled in the past twelve months. The GBI is made up of eight content domains: (1) gambling attitudes (four items), (2) gambling frequency of different games (fifteen), (3) time and money spent gambling (four), (4) gambling frequency at different venues (seven), (5) South Oaks Gambling Screen (twenty-five), (6) DSM-IV diagnostic criteria (ten), (7) research diagnostic items (thirty-two), and (8) demographics (nine items). The DSM-IV items from the GBI were used in the NCAA survey of gambling among college athletes (National Collegiate Athletic Association, 2004).

Implications for College Student Counseling Staff Regarding Prevention and Intervention

Given that a small but significant proportion of college students have a gambling problem, secondary prevention efforts are needed in college settings to help those students identified as problem gamblers, similar to efforts already under way on college campuses with hazardous drinkers. College personnel are in a unique position to provide help to students who are at risk for developing gambling problems. This section outlines a number of services that colleges may offer, such as information and education, screening, referral, and brief interventions.

Awareness, Information, and Education. Doing something is better than nothing; that is, even simple educational materials in the form of pamphlets and literature that may be distributed to college students on how to identify gambling problems and access help on the campus or in the community may be a good place to start. These materials can be distributed at new student orientation, or imbedded in health education provided in medical and mental health centers on campus, with other literature on common high-risk behaviors such as heavy drinking and substance abuse. Awareness and education for the general student body should focus on guidelines for responsible gambling. Abstinence from gambling is the only way to completely avoid risk, but if the student chooses to gamble he or she needs to place limits on time and money spent gambling. Also, information can be disseminated about warning signs of problem gambling, including excessive time and money spent gambling, skipping classes to gamble, gambling when the student should be studying or sleeping, to name a few.

Screening. Lesieur and colleagues (1991) suggested that all college students who come to the counseling center for mental health problems be screened for problem gambling. University medical clinics and counseling centers might embed questions about gambling problems in their standard mental health screening, along with questions about smoking, drinking, drug use, and other high-risk behaviors. Another tack would be to administer brief screening tools, such as the aforementioned SOGS, as a routine part of intake and history gathering at these college care settings.

Referral. Counseling personnel should, at a minimum, furnish information on community resources that are available to help students who are identified as problem gamblers. Community resources include gambling help lines, Gamblers Anonymous (GA) meetings, and professional counseling services.

Treatment. Studies on youth gambling indicate that problem gambling is usually part of a constellation of related problems, including antisocial behavior, alcohol and other drug use, and attention and learning problems, to name a few (Gupta and Derevensky, 1998). Treatment methods used with young problem gamblers are similar to the approaches used with adults (for example, cognitive-behavioral treatments) with some changes to accommodate developmental issues. It is too early to make any conclusions about what treatment is most appropriate or most effective for college students.

That said, designated student counseling staff could learn how to administer brief intervention strategies to help college students with gambling problems. Examples of brief treatment strategies have been outlined by Takushi and others (2004) and Ladouceur, Sylvain, and Boutin (2000). Takushi and associates developed a brief one-session intervention strategy and have written a manual describing how to administer this treatment. The strategy, designed specifically for college students, integrates cognitive behavioral skills training and motivational interviewing including personalized normative feedback, cognitive correction, discussion of gambling consequences, and relapse prevention techniques. The intervention has shown promise in reducing high-risk gambling among college students. In addition, Ladouceur, Sylvain, and Boutin (2000) outlined a brief-intervention strategy for assessing and treating problem gambling, which may be a good strategy for working with college students identified as problem gamblers. First, the SOGS is used to identify those students who are PPG. If the SOGS is positive, a semistructured interview is employed to identify the nature and history of the gambling problem (triggers, nature, extent, consequences of gambling behavior). Because of the high prevalence of substance abuse, anxiety, and depression in pathological gamblers, Ladouceur, Sylvain, and Boutin (2000) also recommend that therapists use additional questionnaires and the interview to determine the relationship between gambling and other co-morbid problems. Ladouceur and colleagues suggest a cognitive behavioral treatment approach aimed at correcting misconceptions about the basic notion of randomness. The cognitive correction includes helping the pathological gambler understand the concepts of randomness, erroneous beliefs, inaccurate perceptions that dominate one's thinking while gambling, and how to question the validity of various erroneous thoughts. This approach may take fifteen or so meetings with the college student and may be better suited to those who have more serious problems with gambling, as well as with those with comorbid substance abuse, anxiety, or depression.

Summary, Conclusions, and Recommendations

Today's college students are the first generation of youths to grow up in a culture of widespread legalized gambling and its promotion (Shaffer, Hall, Vander Bilt, and George, 2003). Yet few colleges have student policies or services regarding gambling (Shaffer and others, 2005). With this in mind, we offer these recommendations for practitioners at colleges and universities:

• Monitor college student gambling behavior, including extent of gambling, illegal gambling, and problem gambling.
• Develop student policies for gambling that emphasize rehabilitation rather than punishment (Shaffer and others, 2005).
• Conduct research into the cause, development, maintenance, and cessation of problem gambling, with an emphasis on risk and protective factors.
• Develop and evaluate prevention programs and messages designed specifically for college students.
• Provide treatment services for students who have already developed a gambling problem.

Regarding the last two recommendations, prevention efforts aimed at a general college student population may primarily teach guidelines for money and time spent gambling. Young adults need to be given information and offered appropriate resources to help them make healthy and informed decisions about gambling. Some students may only need information to assist them in making decisions about gambling, while other students will require more intensive prevention and intervention efforts, in part because they are already gambling in excess and experiencing adverse consequences. These students require more individually tailored prevention and intervention approaches, such as brief cognitive-behavioral interventions. It makes sense to establish a continuum of services on the college campus, including public awareness, prevention, assessment, brief interventions, referrals (help line, treatment in the community, and GA), and on-campus gambling treatment services.

We have made significant inroads in recognizing and understanding gambling and problem gambling among college students. As researchers and college student personnel staff continue attending closely to issues discussed in this chapter, the overall health, well-being, and personal and academic development of college students will be improved.

References

American Psychiatric Association. *Diagnostic and Statistical Manual of Mental Disorders* (4th ed.). Washington, D.C.: APA, 1994.

Baboushkin, H. R., Hardoon, K. K., Derevensky, J. L., and Gupta, R. "Underlying Cognitions in Gambling Behavior Among University Students." *Journal of Applied Social Psychology,* 2001, *31,* 1409–1430.

Breen, R. B., and Zuckerman, M. "'Chasing' in Gambling Behavior: Personality and Cognitive Determinants." *Personality and Individual Differences,* 1999, *27,* 1097–1111.

Clark, D. "Gambling and the Trait of Addition in a Sample of New Zealand University Students." *New Zealand Journal of Psychology,* 2003, *32,* 39–48.

Engwall, D., Hunter, R., and Steinberg, M. "Gambling and Other Risk Behaviors on University Campuses." *Journal of American College Health*, 2004, *52*, 245–255.

Giacopassi, D., Stitt, B. G., and Vandiver, M. "An Analysis of the Relationship of Alcohol to Casino Gambling Among College Students." *Journal of Gambling Studies*, 1998, *14*, 135–149.

Gupta, R., and Derevensky, J. "An Empirical Examination of Jacob's General Theory of Addictions: Do Adolescent Gamblers Fit the Theory?" *Journal of Gambling Studies*, 1998, *14*, 17–49.

Kweitel, R., and Allen, F.C.L. "Cognitive Processes Associated with Gambling Behaviour." *Psychological Reports*, 1998, *82*, 147–153.

LaBrie, R. A., Shaffer, H. J., LaPlante, D. A., and Wechsler, H. "Correlates of College Student Gambling in the United States." *Journal of American College Health*, 2003, *52*, 53–62.

Ladouceur, R., Dube, D., and Bujold, A. "Gambling Among Primary School Students." *Journal of Gambling Studies*, 1994a, *10*, 363–370.

Ladouceur, R., Dube, D., and Bujold, A. "Prevalence of Pathological Gambling and Related Problems Among College Students in the Quebec Metropolitan Area." *Canadian Journal of Psychology*, 1994b, *39*, 289–293.

Ladouceur, R., Sylvain, C., and Boutin, C. "Pathological Gambling." In M. Hersen and M. Biaggio (eds.), *Effective Brief Therapies: A Clinician's Guide*. New York: Academic Press, 2000.

Langewisch, M.W.J., and Frisch, G. R. "Gambling Behavior and Pathology in Relation to Impulsivity, Sensation Seeking, and Risky Behavior in Male College Students." *Journal of Gambling Studies*, 1998, *14*, 245–262.

Lesieur, H. R., and Blume, S. B. "The South Oaks Gambling Screen (SOGS): A New Instrument for the Identification of Pathological Gamblers." *American Journal of Psychiatry*, 1987, *144*, 1184–1188.

Lesieur, H. R., Cross, J., Frank, M., Welch, M., White, C. M., Rubenstein, G., Mosely, K., and Mark, M. "Gambling and Pathological Gambling Among University Students." *Addictive Behaviors*, 1991, *16*, 517–527.

National Collegiate Athletic Association. *2003 NCAA National Study on Collegiate Sports Wagering and Associated Behaviors*. Indianapolis, Ind.: NCAA, 2004.

National Research Council. *Pathological Gambling: A Critical Review*. Washington, D.C.: National Academy Press, 1999.

Neighbors, C., and Larimer, M. E. "Self-Determination and Problem Gambling Among College Students." *Journal of Social and Clinical Psychology*, 2004, *23*, 565–583.

Neighbors, C., Lostutter, T. W., Cronce, J. M., and Larimer, M. E. "Exploring College Student Gambling Motivation." *Journal of Gambling Studies*, 2002, *18*, 361–370.

Platz, L., Knapp, T. J., and Crossman, E. W. "Gambling by Underage College Students: Preferences and Pathology." *College Student Journal*, 2005, *39*, 3–4.

Shaffer, H. J., Donato, A. N., LaBrie, R. A., Kidman, R. C., and LaPlante, D. A. "The Epidemiology of College Alcohol and Gambling Policies." *Harm Reduction Journal*, 2005, *2*, 1–20.

Shaffer, H. J., Hall, M. N., and Vander Bilt, J. *Estimating the Prevalence of Disordered Gambling Behavior in the United States and Canada: A Meta-Analysis*. Boston: Presidents and Fellows of Harvard College, 1997.

Shaffer, H. J., Hall, M. N., Vander Bilt, J., and George, E. (eds.). *Futures at Stake: Youth, Gambling, and Society*. Reno: University of Nevada Press, 2003.

Stinchfield, R. "Gambling and Correlates of Gambling Among Minnesota Public School Students." *Journal of Gambling Studies*, 2000, *16*, 153–173.

Stinchfield, R. "Reliability, Validity, and Classification Accuracy of the South Oaks Gambling Screen (SOGS)." *Addictive Behaviors*, 2002, *27*, 1–19.

Stinchfield, R. "Reliability, Validity, and Classification Accuracy of a Measure of DSM-IV Diagnostic Criteria for Pathological Gambling." *American Journal of Psychiatry,* 2003, *160,* 180–182.

Stinchfield, R. "Demographic, Psychosocial, and Behavioral Factors Associated with Youth Gambling and Problem Gambling." In J. Derevensky and R. Gupta (eds.), *Gambling Problems in Youth: Theoretical and Applied Perspectives.* New York: Kluwer Academic/Plenum, 2004.

Stinchfield, R., Govoni, R., and Frisch, R. G. "Screening and Assessment Instruments." In J. E. Grant and M. N. Potenza (eds.), *Pathological Gambling: A Clinical Guide to Treatment.* Washington, D.C.: American Psychiatric, 2004.

Stinchfield, R., Govoni, R., and Frisch, R. G. "DSM-IV Diagnostic Criteria for Pathological Gambling: Reliability, Validity, and Classification Accuracy." *American Journal on Addictions,* 2005, *14,* 73–82.

Stinchfield, R., and Winters, K. C. "Adolescents and Young Adults." In J. E. Grant and M. N. Potenza (eds.), *Pathological Gambling: A Clinical Guide to Treatment* (pp. 69–81). Washington, D.C.: American Psychiatric, 2004.

Takushi, R. Y., Neighbors, C., Larimer, M. E., Lostutter, T. W., Cronce, J. M., and Marlatt, G. A. "Indicated Prevention of Problem Gambling Among College Students." *Journal of Gambling Studies,* 2004, *20,* 83–93.

Welte, J. W., Barnes, G. M., Wieczorek, W. F., Tidwell, M-C. O., and Parker, J. C. "Risk Factors for Pathological Gambling." *Addictive Behaviors,* 2004, *29,* 323–335.

Winters, K. C., Bengston, P., Dorr, D., and Stinchfield, R. "Prevalence and Risk Factors of Problem Gambling Among College Students." *Psychology of Addictive Behaviors,* 1998, *12,* 127–135.

Winters, K. C., Stinchfield, R., and Kim, L. "Monitoring Adolescent Gambling in Minnesota." *Journal of Gambling Studies,* 1995, *11,* 165–184.

RANDY STINCHFIELD is associate director of the Center for Adolescent Substance Abuse Research in the Department of Psychiatry at the University of Minnesota Medical School.

WILLIAM E. HANSON is a faculty member in the APA-accredited Counseling Psychology Program in the Department of Educational Studies at Purdue University.

DOUGLAS H. OLSON is board-certified in counseling psychology and is director of the Alcohol Related Disease Clinic and the Anxiety Interventions Clinic at the Minneapolis VA Medical Center.

7

This chapter suggests important questions useful in the process of developing or refining institutional or departmental gambling policies. Ethical, political, and social considerations are discussed and then briefly synthesized into three potential policy applications.

Ethical and Practical Considerations for Developing Institutional Gambling Policy

Jason A. Laker

For better or worse, gambling has been a form of leisure and enterprise throughout human history. Thus, its presence in the lives of college students is not a new phenomenon (see the discussion by McClellan and Winters in Chapter One). However, institutions of higher education have yet to show a coherent or effective response to this issue, placing individual students and organizations at risk.

This chapter extends general guidance toward development, refinement, and enforcement of institutional or departmental gambling policies. Although it is intended to offer practical advice and conceptual frameworks for policy formation, the reader is advised that gambling, like many other societal issues, is much more complex than it appears at first blush. Thus the chapter begins with a number of questions that can stimulate useful discussion, debate, and ideally movement toward consensus among stakeholders engaged in development of a gambling policy at the institutional or departmental level. The chapter then focuses on ethical, philosophical, and practical considerations in framing campus discussion and making decisions about gambling policy. Finally, three possible institutional frameworks are explored in light of the questions and considerations that have been identified.

NEW DIRECTIONS FOR STUDENT SERVICES, no. 113, Spring 2006   © Wiley Periodicals, Inc.
Published online in Wiley InterScience (www.interscience.wiley.com) • DOI: 10.1002/ss.197

Beginning Questions

In preparing to engage the campus in a discussion of campus gambling, it is advisable to begin by exploring the answers to a number of questions that may serve to inform the larger discussion.

Defining Gambling. Chapter One of this volume is an extended discussion of various ways in which gambling might be defined. To craft an effective policy or approach regarding gambling, it is critically important to develop a consensus on the institution's working definition. Similarly, it is important to decide whether the institution will view a student engaging in a particular activity differently than it would an employee, department, or official student organization.

Depending on one's tendency toward wordsmithing, it is possible that establishing a working definition will actually be fairly easy for the purposes of setting policy. A century ago, Hobson (1905) defined gambling quite simply as being "the determination of the ownership of property by appeal to chance. By chance is here implied the resultant of a play of natural forces that cannot be controlled or calculated by those who appeal to it" (p. 10). By this definition, everything from online wagering, bingo, or playing cards to purchasing raffle or lottery tickets constitutes gambling. Whether this particular definition is appealing or not, it is important to establish an official definition in order to be clear and avoid inconsistent situational and subjective enforcement.

Whereas Hobson's definition includes virtually every possible activity, one large state university takes an interesting approach to this exercise. Rather than defining gambling according to a dictionary per se, it explicitly defines it relative to legality:

> "Gambling" means any illegal betting, including but not limited to: wagering on or selling pools on any athletic or other event; possessing on one's person or premises (room, residence unit, car), or in a computer account or electronic format, any card, book or other device for registering bets; knowingly using or permitting the use of one's premises or one's telephone or other electronic communications device for illegal gambling; knowingly receiving or delivering a letter, package or parcel or electronic or telephonic communication related to illegal gambling; offering, soliciting or accepting a bribe to influence the outcome of an athletic event; and involvement in bookmaking or wagering pools with respect to sporting events [University of Arizona, 2005].

After defining the term *gambling,* this institution prohibits two specific activities relative to this definition: "off-campus conduct related to gambling associated with any university event or activity," and "gambling as prohibited by law or applicable policy" (University of Arizona, 2005). The philosophical position embedded within this approach is discussed in more detail later. Suffice it to say here that institutions would be best served by defining their use of the term *gambling* as clearly and succinctly as possible within their policy. There are minor stylistic considerations as well. Some student codes or employee handbooks define terms in one section, and then list prohibited activities in another. Others blend definitions and prohibitions together. Regardless, consistency and congruence are advised.

Other Questions. How, if at all, does location (on or off-campus; residence hall or student union; Greek house; via the institution's telephones, intranet, or Internet service provider; on study abroad, service trips, or bordering countries) mitigate how or when the institution defines or enforces its policy? What if a perfectly legal and acceptable activity is planned, but the planners fail to submit particular forms or hold meetings explicitly required under the policy? Will all or certain gambling activities or businesses be allowed to advertise on campus, in official publications, or in the student paper?

Finally, will it be expected that the development or alumni affairs office, athletic boosters, and president's office abide by the same expectations as student services offices, individual students, or student clubs? It is important to thoughtfully consider the many questions posed in this chapter as policy discussion progresses. This is because, as most administrators can appreciate, such questions are likely to be raised eventually—often at an unfortunate, embarrassing, or inconvenient time.

Ethical, Philosophical, and Practical Considerations

In addition to the important questions discussed earlier, there are some other decisions to be made and obligations to fulfill in establishing a sound policy. Obviously, one set of considerations pertains to local, state, and national laws. Regardless of institutional mission or philosophy, it is important for administrators, faculty, and students to be aware of laws pertaining directly or indirectly to gambling, as well as the institution's policy on gambling. Of course, the purview and status of each community member (faculty and staff in general as opposed to judicial officers; students in general, or club officers) will inform how versed they should be. This knowledge is especially important to those working in student activities, Greek affairs, athletics, and residence life as well as to faculty who serve as advisors. It may also be useful to apprise business officers who process expenditures, since they are likely to catch requisitions and purchase orders for products and services that are themselves legal but violate institutional policy.

Beyond the obvious expectation that the institution will remain in compliance with the law, there are political and social considerations that are inescapable. For instance, institutional mission is often invoked to support a particular position. This is just as true for public institutions as it is for religious ones. Thus, in deciding who will participate in policy formation (and consequently who will not), one must consider the current climate for the discussion, both on and off campus. If there has not been a recent and serious conversation about the mission and its implications, or perhaps even if there has, the subject of gambling may provoke strong sentiments. Critical constituent groups such as the faculty or student senate may have strong opinions about gambling, and these positions may be disparate or even unlawful. One must be prepared for this and choose battles wisely.

Off campus, the state legislature or federal government may be embroiled in debate on the issue, or perhaps a critical incident involving gambling has recently occurred. Perhaps a potential donor has some relationship to a gambling enterprise, or maybe the religious denomination with which the institution is affiliated holds a strong (or even a vague) position on the subject. The institution's geographic proximity to a casino or other gambling venue will naturally affect the practicality of certain policy positions as well. However, with the proliferation of off-shore and Web-based gambling, local businesses are not the only venues to be taken into account in policy planning.

These are but some of the influences on policy formation in general, and for our purposes gambling policy in particular. To relieve the reader of a potentially overwhelming feeling provoked by the litany of considerations presented in this chapter, remember that risk is not something that can be entirely prevented. Rather, it is something to be managed. Consequently, seek to create a policy that is lawful, reasonable, and understandable. Good intentions and due diligence can go a long way. Hobson (1905) wisely offered that "even a moral order imposed in the public interest, if too uniform and rigorous, will arouse, not merely in bad but in good natures, reactions toward lawlessness" (p. 142).

First, Do No Harm; . . . Second, Try to Help

In addition to establishing a gambling policy that regulates such activities, it is important to demonstrate care for the health and welfare of students, faculty, and staff. Institutions should be prepared to prevent, defuse, or help resolve problems stemming from gambling activities (addiction, interpersonal conflicts, violence). More will be said later about the notion of prevention within the context of three philosophical approaches. In the meantime, consider this statement included in the gambling policy at a small, private, religious institution: "Students voluntarily seeking assistance for a gambling-related problem may do so without fear of disciplinary action, and will be treated with the utmost sensitivity and confidentiality. Such assistance may be sought through a residence hall staff member; the Residential Life Office; Health Services; the Counseling and Testing Services; Campus Ministry; and the Office of the Vice President for Student Life" (Pacific Lutheran University, 2005).

NEW DIRECTIONS FOR STUDENT SERVICES • DOI 10.1002/ss

This institution offers amnesty for students who come forward prior to being confronted for a violation and indicates whom to approach with a request. Saint Martin's University (2004) articulates a willingness to offer resources and gives more detail about the services to be offered, but it does not offer amnesty: "Counseling is available for students with gambling or other addictive or problematic habits to identify and assess concerns, identify relevant goals, and assist with appropriate interventions and/or support resources."

There will be concrete implications of any policy for those who enforce it, as well as for those who offer support services. Therefore it is wise to include security and police officers, residential life staff, health educators, ministry, and counseling staff in discussions about gambling policies, and ensure that they are prepared to identify warning signs and responses to gambling-related problems.

Another important topic to be discussed relative to harm reduction and student support is how assessment and institutional research programs include gambling attitudes and behaviors, and how they connect to campus climate and student experience. It may be useful to collect certain baseline data prior to developing a policy, or to establish an interim policy while such data are being gathered. Many institutions conduct surveys related to health and wellness issues such as alcohol, sleep, exercise, nutrition, and the like, but perhaps not about gambling. Since a gambling policy or particular incidents may create controversy, having good data can be quite helpful. Similarly, funding for student support services or planning and training ought to be informed by such data.

Beyond that, measuring improvement or reduction in gambling-related problems, or even determining a relationship between gambling and certain student issues (such as alcohol or drug abuse, violence, or poor academic performance) or demography (such as race or gender), cannot be accomplished without sound assessment and research practices. It is important to note that surveying can be (or can become) political (Schuh and Upcraft, 2000), whether because of social conventions, subject matter, risk and litigation, or personalities in key leadership positions. Thus it is advisable to have the input and support of senior administrators whose work is affected by these dynamics or who influence such dynamics.

Implications: Three Policy Positions

A significant set of considerations have been offered for use in the process of developing gambling policies. As stakeholders grapple with these questions, define terms, and contemplate the costs, benefits, and logistical application of policies, an institutional or departmental position on the issue will become clearer. To assist in this synthesis, three plausible viewpoints are discussed, as well as some related assumptions and implications.

NEW DIRECTIONS FOR STUDENT SERVICES • DOI 10.1002/ss

Zero Tolerance. This position assumes that gambling ought not to be allowed for religious, ethical, liability, or educational reasons. One small, private, religiously affiliated institution with such a policy articulates it thus: "Gambling is not permitted on campus. Neither is gambling permitted in connection with college-sponsored events off campus. This means that lotteries, raffles and similar games of chance are not to be conducted either on or off campus by [institution] organizations, departments or groups. While [institution] organizations, departments or groups are not allowed to sell chances to win a prize, this policy does not preclude auctions or giving away door prizes in connection with an event if the admission ticket is not sold as a chance to win something" [Concordia College, 1997].

This policy is succinct, and it defines behaviors that are prohibited and allowed by individuals and groups. There is always the possibility for debate about certain elements, but it is reasonably straightforward. Since this is a private institution, it has a good deal of latitude in regulating student behavior, even if such behavior is not precluded by law.

Moderate or Semiregulatory. This position assumes either that gambling is acceptable in moderation, or that there are practical limits to the amount of control the institution can or should exercise. This may mean that gambling activities are allowed but nothing of monetary value can be required or exchanged, or it may allow such exchange so long as it is within the parameters established by law. One large private institution has an interesting approach that fits within this position, and that may be workable for a public institution in consultation with its legal counsel:

> It is [institution] policy that any event which suggests University endorsement of gambling is not permissible. Given the broad definition of "gambling" under [state] law, any "game of chance or skill" is an act of gambling when played "for money or other thing of value." This definition encompasses blackjack, poker and euchre, as well as any other card game, craps, roulette, and other comparable games when these games are played for money or any other thing of value (including prizes). If prizes are awarded at all at an event where games of chance or skill are being played, there is still a strong possibility that the event could be construed as a gambling event in violation of [state] law. As long as the event is not marketed as a Vegas Night, Casino Night, or Poker Night and nothing of value, including money and/or prizes, exchanges hands, then game and/or card nights may be allowed for student organizations. Events featuring bona fide games of skill, such as darts or billiards, at which prizes are awarded, may be permissible, but betting will not be allowed. Any requests for events at which games of skill will be played must be approved by the Center for Student Involvement [Northwestern University, 2004].

Of particular note in this policy is the first sentence, which reaches beyond local laws and prohibits gambling activities that may suggest the school endorses the behavior. It also assigns the authority for making such a determination. Finally, it attends to potentially vague and problematic aspects of that state's laws. Although there are workable gambling policies that allow any lawful activity, this particular one was included here because it is inventive in its capacity to protect the institution and its authority, and yet offer reasonable parameters within a specific policy position.

Another school, in this case a moderate-sized public institution, maintains a policy that allows lawful gambling but regulates elements of its planning and execution:

> Campus organizations may request, through the Office of Student Union and Activities, to sponsor a free Las Vegas or casino night on the campus. An organization member must meet with a representative of the Office of Student Union and Activities well in advance (several months) of the event to review the legal and procedural restrictions on such events. Representatives from the following areas will be in attendance during this initial event planning meeting: sponsoring groups; Office of Student Union and Activities; University Police; and Food Services if applicable. During the initial event planning meeting, decisions will be made regarding the logistics for the event. No publicity may be prepared for or contracts entered into without prior event authorization from the Office of Student Union and Activities. Sponsoring organizations should plan to hold 3–4 event planning meetings with a representative of the Office of Student Union and Activities. An individual organization may sponsor only one "free casino night" per academic year.
>
> The sponsoring organization must comply with all provisions of campus policies and state and federal laws concerning casino parties; in particular, information detailed in Sections [number] through [number] of the [state code] which pertains to Gaming. No person under the age of 18 is permitted. The event must be open to all members of the campus community, except those under the age of 18. There can be no entrance or advance registration fee. Scrip or chips must be used for play; no money can be used. Scrip must be distributed free with no connection to any voluntary donation. All volunteers must wear identification chest-high throughout the event. Prior to advertising for a Casino Night, a member from the sponsoring organization must have already met with a representative of the Office of Student Union and Activities to discuss the procedures for handling such an activity. Organizations must scrupulously abide by these and the state's regulations. Failure to comply will result in event termination, possible campus sanctions and/or criminal prosecution [California State University, Dominguez Hills, 2004].

The reader can likely understand why the word *arguably* was used to describe the fit of this policy with a moderate position. The author cites this policy as a cautionary tale. Gambling activities are technically allowed, but this policy includes so many detailed requirements as to be minimally off-putting to students, if not provocative. Of particular concern is that it places the student activities staff in an adversarial and intrusive position relative to students, and it could potentially undermine a vibrant social climate or perhaps increase preventable judicial hearings. In fairness to the institution, certain states or central system offices impose complex requirements on individual institutions.

No Comment or Endorsement. The no-endorsement position not only allows all legal forms of gambling but also includes sponsorship or organizing of such activities. Not surprisingly, the author was unable to locate an institutional gambling policy that explicitly encourages gambling. Rather, this position describes an approach in which there is no expressed policy relative to gambling, and one or more gambling activities are actively encouraged. For instance, one private, liberal arts institution has held an annual gambling event for almost forty years. It has become a powerful tradition, raising funds for charity and attracting significant participation within the campus community. Whether this is positive or negative, benign or harmful can be left to the reader or researcher. Nonetheless, this position can have the effect of institutionally encouraging or endorsing gambling activities.

A related approach within this position could perhaps be referred to as the "no harm, no foul" position. Accordingly, an institution may not have a specified gambling policy but retains some capacity to step in when trouble arises. For instance, one small, private, religiously affiliated institution has this language in its student code:

> Students are accountable for ordinary standards of behavior even though particular misconduct may not be explicitly mentioned in University documents. The University reserves the right to deny admission, continued enrollment, re-enrollment, or to apply disciplinary sanctions to any applicant or student whose personal history, background, or behavior, indicate that his/her presence at the University or University functions or activities would endanger the health, safety, welfare, or property of the members of the University community or interfere with the orderly and effective performance of the University's functions [Saint John's University, 2005].

This policy gives the institution broad authority to regulate student behavior deemed problematic by its officials. Since it is private, and students agree to the terms of the student code by merely enrolling, it is legally defensible. Nonetheless, such a policy, if invoked more often than student, parent, or faculty comfort allows, could cause significant conflict.

Regardless of which philosophy ultimately informs a particular institution's policy, it is essential that there be congruence between institutional mission, philosophy, policy, and enforcement. This in turn reduces the possibility of confusion, perceived or real duplicity, risk exposure, harm, or student resentment. Even institutions whose mission suggests or explicitly regards gambling as dangerous or immoral ought to have a well-defined policy that articulates precisely what activities are or are not acceptable, and the reasons for same.

Disseminating Policy. In addition to determining a specific gambling policy, it is important to publicize and disseminate it for use by campus constituents. The student code and employee handbook may be the most obvious places to publish the policy. In addition, the institution may choose to make mention of the policy in club recognition materials and sample constitutions. If the institution prohibits certain off-campus participation in gambling activities, then the transportation policy (including those pertaining specifically to study abroad, recreational, and service trips) and related contracts are other places for comment on this issue. Residence hall and Greek house contracts should also specify prohibited gambling activities. It may also be useful to consider whether computer and network use policies ought to include language regarding online gambling. In all cases, it is worth consulting an attorney about precise language to be used, as well as about whether no or limited policy is preferable to creating a potentially cumbersome or unenforceable policy.

Summary

This chapter focuses on the mechanics of a process for creating gambling policies. Clearly, there are additional issues worthy of consideration and future research. For example, it is within the liberal learning tradition to deeply reflect on ethical and philosophical issues associated with gambling. How does an institution's policy attend not just to legal considerations but also to the very purpose of higher education? What ideologies are embedded within such policies? Is the institution complicit in one or more systems of stratification or exploitation? As a social scientist given to critical theory, the author finds such questions compelling. However, as a college administrator, the author recognizes that decisions must be made and defended.

As the name of this volume (and history) suggests, it is likely just a matter of time before institutions are mandated to establish, disseminate, and enforce gambling policies. If institutions of higher education enact leadership on this issue, then the regulatory efforts forthcoming can be more thoughtfully developed, less costly and intrusive, and more effective.

References

California State University, Dominguez Hills. "Casino Night Policy." 2004. http://www.csudh.edu/srr/casino.htm; accessed Nov. 17, 2005.

Concordia College. "Student Life Policies." 1997. http://www.cord.edu/dept/registrar/catalog97/studentlifepolicies.html#gamb; accessed Nov. 17, 2005.

Hobson, J. "The Ethics of Gambling." *International Journal of Ethics,* 1905, *15*(2), 135–148.

Northwestern University. "Student Organization Gambling Policy." 2004. http://www.norris.northwestern.edu/images/Gambling_Policy.doc; accessed Nov. 17, 2005.

Pacific Lutheran University. "Student Code of Conduct 2005–06." 2005. http://www.plu.edu/print/handbook/code-of-conduct/gambling.html; accessed Nov. 17, 2005.

Saint John's University. "Behavior." 2005. http://www.csbsju.edu/jbook/policies/behavior.htm; accessed Nov. 17, 2005.

Saint Martin's University. "Gambling Policies." 2004. http://www.stmartin.edu/security/Policies/gambling.htm; accessed Dec. 28, 2005.

Schuh, J., and Upcraft, M. "Assessment Politics." *About Campus,* 2000, *5,* 14–21.

University of Arizona. "Student Code of Conduct." 2005. http://dos.web.arizona.edu/uapolicies/scc5308e.html; accessed Nov. 17, 2005.

JASON A. LAKER is dean of campus life at Saint John's University and an adjunct faculty member there and at St. Cloud State University.

This chapter relates the experiences of one university in developing and implementing a cross-divisional proactive program to address campus gambling. Insights and recommendations for similar efforts on other campuses are also shared.

The Gambling Action Team: A Cross-Divisional Approach to Gambling Education and Intervention

Chris King, Thomas W. Hardy

Developing and implementing a gambling action team (or, alternatively, panel or committee) is a proactive approach that institutions can use to facilitate education and intervention regarding campus gambling. This chapter describes the development and implementation of the Gambling Action Team (GAT) at the University of Alabama. The chapter opens with a discussion of the context in which the need for a gambling education and intervention program at the university was identified and the framework within which formulation of the GAT took place. Next, the development process for the GAT is recounted. Planning and programming by the GAT are then shared, as are plans for assessing the impact of the GAT's work. The chapter concludes with insights and recommendations for consideration by other campuses interested in developing a gambling education and intervention program.

Context and Framework

As a result of its interaction with the National Collegiate Athletic Association (NCAA), the Athletic Department at the University of Alabama was involved in gambling education and intervention for student athletes. Given the interaction between student athletes and the student body at large, and given concerns regarding the growing popularity of gambling

among college students, members of the Athletic Department approached colleagues across campus in the spring of 2003 about expanding gambling education and intervention efforts across campus.

The provost and interim vice president for student affairs then charged the Gambling Action Team to develop a campuswide comprehensive program for gambling education and intervention. The authors of this chapter, who at the time served in the Athletic Department and Residential Life at the University of Alabama, were asked to serve as the first cochairs of the Gambling Action Team. As we began our work with the GAT, we did not see our purpose as being to oppose gambling behavior per se but rather to promote compliance with applicable laws and policies, moderation of gambling activity, and early identification and intervention for students who are at risk for problem gambling.

Development of the GAT

The cochairs worked to identify specific members of the students, staff, and faculty to be invited to serve on the GAT. Contacting potential members about joining the GAT was an opportunity to gauge interest in gambling issues across campus.

The university's Gambling Action Team comprises student members appointed by the Student Government Association and the Inter-Fraternity Council. It also includes staff and faculty from the Division of Student Affairs, Counseling Center, Office of the Dean of Students, Russell Health Center, UA Police Department, University Relations, Human Resources, various academic departments, and Intercollegiate Athletics.

As cochairs of the GAT, we felt one of our first priorities should be to better educate ourselves and members of the GAT regarding campus gambling problems and best practices in addressing campus gambling. Although we found little information on the latter, we did learn that Florida State University (FSU) had a Gambling Action Team in place. After discussion with the chair of FSU's GAT, we received numerous materials that served as a helpful starting point in our efforts. We are pleased to take this opportunity to publicly acknowledge our appreciation for the pioneering work of the FSU GAT, and we hope that our willingness to share our experiences at the University of Alabama will be as helpful to the effort of others as FSU's generosity has been helpful to our institution's efforts.

Planning and Programming

During the 2003–04 academic year, the GAT developed a set of strategic priorities that were later reviewed and approved by the provost and vice president for student affairs. The GAT's priorities included (1) developing a comprehensive gambling education program for the student body, faculty, and staff; (2) providing consultation services to the student body on problem gambling and debt management; (3) developing an approach to raise awareness regarding problem gambling, as well as gambling- and sports wagering–related issues, on campus; and (4) ensuring compliance with local, state, and federal laws, as well as NCAA legislation.

Planning. Following identification of the four strategic priorities, members of the GAT agreed on four important planning goals:

1. Determine short-term and long-term goals
2. Identify programming to support those goals
3. Identify start-up and continued funding
4. Assess regularly and change as needed

In the preliminary meetings, the GAT established several short- and long-term goals (see the exhibit at the end of this chapter for a listing by strategic priority). The short-term goals included establishing gambling programs and speakers for the student body; distribution of literature to certain segments of the student body, media, and public relations releases through the campus radio, television, and newspaper outlets; and fostering awareness activities throughout campus. The long-term goals included holding a campuswide gambling symposium; researching current gambling studies on the student body focusing on prevalence of gambling on campus, methods used, and the most popular types of gambling; investigation into student gambling, in particular among student athletes and the Greek system; and lastly, providing counseling for students with problems.

With regard to start-up and continued funding, the GAT was not regularly funded by any one unit within the university. Supportive offices contributed money as the need arose, and members of the GAT contributed their time and energy.

Programming. In this section, information is shared about the planning and programming efforts of the University of Alabama's GAT in support of its four strategic priorities.

Developing a Comprehensive Gambling Education Program. The first strategic priority for the GAT was to develop a comprehensive gambling education program for students, staff, and faculty. During the preliminary meetings, the GAT developed consensus around an "informed consumer" approach in its educational programming. In the opinion of the GAT, gambling will continue to take place on college campuses. However, members of the University of Alabama community, particularly its student members, should be informed regarding the potential consequences of engaging in gambling. Specifically, students need to be aware of the potential violation of the student code of conduct; violation of local, state, and federal law; problem gambling issues; debt issues; and, for student-athletes, violation of NCAA legislation and the possibility of loss of eligibility and amateur status.

NEW DIRECTIONS FOR STUDENT SERVICES • DOI 10.1002/ss

The GAT implemented an annual calendar of educational programming sessions. This programming was intended to reach all segments of campus, but the GAT particularly hoped to reach student athletes, members of the Greek system, graduate students, students living in campus residence halls, and staff and faculty with the educational programming.

The cornerstone of the GAT's educational outreach was initiation of a campuswide gambling symposium. The symposium featured individual speakers and panels discussing various aspects of gambling issues. To ensure that symposium audiences received a complete picture of the various aspects of campus gambling, speakers were chosen from a variety of organizations and areas of experience and expertise. Examples were speakers and panelists from the NCAA, FBI, Gamblers Anonymous, National Council on Compulsive Gambling, and former student and student athletes who could share personal experiences as compulsive gamblers or student bookies.

Consultation Services.   Consultation services are a key component for any effective gambling education and intervention program. One of the key partners that must be at the table is the campus counseling center. As the cochairs learned early in exploring the topic, almost no college student enters the counseling center and admits to being addicted to gambling and needing help. In fact, the Counseling Center at the University of Alabama could not even document a case where a student self-identified as having a gambling problem. More often than not, the symptoms were identified first and several sessions ensued before the underlying cause became clear.

By no means should problem gambling among college students be seen as only a concern among the professional counseling staff. Along with the psychological aspects, there are real financial consequences to excessive gambling, and working with debt management is vital. On the University of Alabama campus, the GAT partnered with an assistant dean in the College of Human Environmental Sciences to offer financial counseling for students facing gambling-related financial difficulties.

The GAT also identified consultation resources beyond those available on campus. In Alabama, we rely on the Florida Council for Compulsive Gambling (FCCG), since the state lacks its own phone center for gambling problem consultative services. Every state or region has similar resources, and there are several national resource organizations as well. Readers are referred to the resources list at the end of this volume for detailed information.

Raising Awareness.   To raise awareness of the impact of gambling on the college-age population, it is important to seek out any opportunity to educate the campus in general in some unconventional ways. One was to use existing programs on campus to work awareness of the services GAT provides into the programs. On our campus, we used events such as summer orientation to get the message across in a nonthreatening manner by having students, not an administrator, broach the topic.

The GAT also made significant use of advertising and distribution of literature in its efforts to raise awareness. Key dates for peak gambling—activity such as the Bowl Championship Series and March Madness—were targeted for advertisements in the campus newspaper. One of the ads took a subtle approach and shared resources on campus for students experiencing financial hardship, with no mention of gambling at all. Another ad shared the confidential nature of counseling on campus for gambling concerns as well as a national toll-free help line. The ads were costly, but they assisted in getting the message out to the widest possible audience at the university.

The GAT developed and distributed its "Don't Gamble with Your Future" brochure. This twelve-page color brochure covered the GAT's purpose, contact information, myths of gambling, phases of problem gambling, signs of compulsive gambling, and information on sports wagering, debt management, and sources to receive confidential help or assistance. The brochure was widely distributed to all students during each university orientation session, residence hall check-in, and fraternity and sorority recruitment.

Public service announcements are another method to raise awareness of student gambling. At the University of Alabama, the GAT has asked the campus radio station to make periodic gambling-related public service announcements on air. The GAT also has plans to use the LCD screen at home football and basketball games to display a message of how and where to receive problem gambling assistance.

Finally, the GAT developed a Web site (hosted by the Athletics Department) where we made available our brochures, copies of presentations, information on upcoming programs, and sources for assistance with problem gambling. The GAT also furnishes information on recent research related to campus gambling on the Web site.

Developing University Gambling Policies. The GAT reviewed the Code of Student Conduct, Housing and Residential Communities Handbook, and regulations of national fraternities and sororities with regard to gambling. They found that the UA documents addressed gambling, and many of the national fraternities and sororities had policies prohibiting members from engaging in campus gambling.

In the course of review of University of Alabama policies regarding gambling, it was learned that there was no specific mention of gambling in the staff and faculty handbooks. The GAT intends to address this issue through the respective governing bodies. Employees and faculty associates of the Athletics Department were subject to applicable NCAA regulations, which prohibit participation in sports wagering on intercollegiate or professional athletics and offer information concerning intercollegiate athletics to individuals involved in gambling (National Collegiate Athletic Association, 2003).

Unanticipated Opportunities. One of the main issues the Gambling Action Team at the University of Alabama was faced with was the fact that gambling, even in a predominantly nongambling state, is pervasive in our culture. The GAT encountered three instances of campus departments or affiliates using gambling to attract students to programs and activities.

University Recreation had planned advertising a Texas Hold 'Em tournament in the spring semester. A member of the GAT spoke to the director of the unit regarding the potentially conflicting messages that might be sent by sponsoring such an alternative within the recreation complex. To the director's credit, the brief conversation immediately sparked an interest in reconsidering such an activity even on the intramural level, and the tournaments were discontinued as they were determined to not be a part of an overall healthy campus.

Another example was not as easy to solve. The student newspaper *The Crimson White* ran several lead articles on the subject of gambling and poker during the academic year in question. The newspaper ran articles regarding the winners of Internet poker, a local bar offering live poker for prizes, and the vagueness of enforcement of ordinances related to private gambling in homes. To make matters worse, the *Crimson White* reported an article on a former UA student who dropped out of college to play online poker and claimed to have won over $40,000. This article appeared the same day as the GAT's Gambling Symposium. In light of concerns for freedom of the press, the best intervention was to ask the *Crimson White* to publish some stories on the potential risks of gambling as well. As a result, on two separate occasions the *Crimson White* reported on the Gambling Action Team's purpose and activities.

Assessment

The plan of action for the UA Gambling Action Team began during the 2004–05 academic year. Goals and objectives were initiated and will continue through the growth of this plan, with ongoing review and improvements made where deemed appropriate throughout the life of the plan. This is a dynamic document that will grow and change as objectives are completed, as goals are achieved, as the environment changes, and as the education and awareness program grows.

The progress of the plan should be determined by evaluating achievement of the specific short-term and long-term goals outlined within the plan. The cochairs will design an internal action plan to set a schedule for assigning the goals, objectives, and responsibilities for measuring progress and for making necessary adjustments to meet the demands of organizational and environmental changes. A tracking system will be implemented to account for the goals and objectives being completed and achieved in the prescribed time frame. The GAT members will receive copies of the plan for their review at the beginning-of-the-year meeting and follow-up information at monthly and quarterly meetings in regard to the mission, goals, objectives, and vision of the program.

The cochairs have been tasked with reviewing the plan at least annually and furnishing an annual report on the plan's progress to the president, provost, vice president for student affairs, director of athletics, faculty athletics representative, and various university committees. This last part of the assessment plan might be the most important inasmuch as awareness on the part of the university's senior leadership is critically important for continued administrative support and keeping the team intact and focused. By reinforcing what GAT is achieving, inertia will not set in and the team remains encouraged to aim high and accomplish as much as possible.

Conclusion

According to the Connecticut Council on Problem Gambling (1998), a successful gambling prevention program relies on multiple strategies and practices, including strategies from each of these categories: (1) information and awareness (pamphlets, posters, public service announcements, billboards, newsletters); (2) education and skill development (professional development seminars for administrators, faculty, coaches, and staff, and life skills training for student athletes and students); (3) community development, capacity building, and institutional change (engagement of the university community in a targeted gambling reduction prevention plan, and review of the institution's and the Athletics Department's current gambling prevention policy); (4) public and social policy (development and implementation of a gambling policy at the institution); and (5) intervention for individuals at high risk (programs developed by and for at-risk populations, such as student athletes, and development of policies and procedures for referring first-time offenders of institutional gambling policy).

The GAT preparation and implementation of a gambling education, awareness, and treatment plan of action at the University of Alabama is an example of a comprehensive gambling prevention program on a college campus. From our experience to date with the GAT at the University of Alabama, we offer several insights and recommendations for others considering implementing a gambling education and intervention program on their campus.

The planning and implementation of a gambling prevention program demands commitment, vision, time, and resources. Our experience at the University of Alabama leads us to believe it is never too early to begin a gambling prevention program on your campus.

Only through the active participation and cooperation of the members of the university administration, faculty and staff, and intercollegiate athletics will a gambling education and intervention plan succeed in its implementation and goals.

Once established, the GAT members need to be adequately trained to deal with gambling issues as they encounter them. When the GAT at the University of Alabama was established in 2003, we asked our faculty members on the team to present the basics of gambling behavior, asked the Counseling Center representative to address the symptoms and psychological considerations, and asked all members to educate themselves by reviewing pertinent literature on the topic and report back to the group their findings so we could form a consensus of what we wanted to do as a team.

Evaluation of the current university policies as well as applicable state and local law regarding gambling is always a good first step in establishment of a Gambling Action Team.

A key element in the gambling education program is selection of the speaker or speakers who are invited to campus. Be they former compulsive gamblers, students with gambling problems, or FBI agents, it is important that the speaker relate to the audience. The speaker needs to be dynamic and send a powerful message.

For many institutions, one of the best places to incorporate educational materials and discussion on gambling is in their compass or life-skills courses. Topics in the typical freshman course include alcohol, drugs, and sex-related issues, so adding gambling as part of the course is easy and fits well into the curriculum. It allows students, in a safe forum, to get together and talk about what can happen, and have an open discussion with a faculty or staff member.

There are many avenues through which an institution can address student gambling. A comprehensive program that indicates numerous elements is well worth the effort, both to preserve the educational mission of a university and for the welfare of the student body. The important thing is that we not fall prey to the NIMBY syndrome—not in my back yard; gambling can and does occur on college campuses everywhere.

Exhibit: University of Alabama's Gambling Action Team Strategic Priorities and Objectives

Goal 1: Develop a comprehensive gambling education program for the student body and faculty and staff under the direction of the UA Gambling Action Team.

Objective 1: Develop an annual calendar of events for educational sessions each academic year.

Objective 1(a): Develop annual educational sessions for student-athletes.

Objective 1(b): Develop educational sessions to be held each year for the Greek system.

NEW DIRECTIONS FOR STUDENT SERVICES • DOI 10.1002/ss

Objective 1(c): Develop annual educational sessions for the graduate students.

Objective 1(d): Develop educational sessions for the general campus community and residence halls to be presented on an annual basis.

Objective 1(e): Develop annual educational sessions for faculty and staff (including coaches and athletic staff members).

Objective 2: Host a Campus Gambling Symposium each spring.

Objective 3: Provide educational resources and materials for the student body and faculty and staff.

Objective 4: Maintain a gambling link on the athletics compliance Web site (www.rolltide.com).

Objective 5: Secure speakers on an annual basis from the professional sports community, law enforcement, or gambling industry to host educational sessions for the Gambling Action Team.

Goal 2: Provide consultation services to the student body on problem gambling and debt management.

Objective 1: Offer confidential consultative services and assistance for problem gamblers through the Russell Student Health Center.

Objective 2: Make available financial consultative review (debt management) and assistance for students with gambling problems.

Objective 3: Identify local resources for students with gambling problems, including but not limited to forming working relationships with local Gamblers Anonymous groups.

Objective 4: Give Gambling Action Team members and others training and information on gambling problems from outside organizations.

Goal 3: Develop an approach to raise awareness regarding problem gambling and related issues on campus.

Objective 1: Incorporate gambling education and awareness into these programs:

Objective 1(a): First-Year Orientation Program

Objective 1(b): Student Athlete Freshman Life Skills Course

Objective 1(c): General Campus Community and Residence Halls Quarterly Meetings

Objective 1(d): Greek Life Orientation Week and Fraternity New Member Programming

Objective 1(e): Graduate School Orientation Week

Objective 1(f): New Faculty and Staff Orientation

Objective 2: Distribute literature and advertisements outlining the warning signs of gambling, twenty-four-hour contact number, and information on debt management around campus.

Objective 3: Disseminate athletic public service announcements to be shown during home football and men's basketball, and on television during games, by the president, director of athletics, or student athlete(s).

New Directions for Student Services • DOI 10.1002/ss

Objective 4: Partner with the *Crimson White* newspaper on quarterly arti-
cles on gambling during opportune times of year (College Bowl games,
Super Bowl, March Madness).
Objective 5: Use current studies and surveys on student gambling behavior
for education and awareness programs and materials.
Objective 6: Produce an annual assessment report to the president, provost,
and the vice president for student affairs.
Goal 4: Ensure compliance with local, state, and federal laws (and NCAA
rules and regulations).
Objective 1: Develop a Gambling Policy for the following, with inclusion of
the state of Alabama law:
Objective 1(a): Student Code of Conduct
Objective 1(b): Student Athlete Code of Conduct (NCAA rules application)
Objective 1(c): Staff Code of Conduct
Objective 1(d): Faculty Code of Conduct

References

Connecticut Council on Problem Gambling. "Prevention of Problem Gambling." 1998.
http://www.ccpg.org; accessed July 25, 2005.
National Collegiate Athletic Association. *2003–2004 NCAA Division I Manual.*
Indianapolis, Ind.: NCAA, 2003.

*CHRIS KING is associate athletics director in charge of compliance at the
University of Alabama.*

*THOMAS W. HARDY is director of housing and residence life at Valdosta State
University and previously served as cochair of the Gambling Action Team at
the University of Alabama.*

9

*The coeditors of the volume identify seven messages,
address a number of remaining points, and offer summary
comments on where we go from here.*

Learning and Living with the Genie

George S. McClellan, Jim Caswell, Thomas W. Hardy

History and current conditions point us to the conclusion that gambling is
likely to continue to be a part of human culture. It also seems likely that
members of our campus communities, particularly students, will continue to
be engaged in gambling behavior. Some will do so in fairly developmental
and transient ways, but others in ways that are sustained, intense, and sometimes destructive to themselves, those around them, and their institutions.

The authors of this volume have offered us information regarding a
variety of aspects of campus gambling, and there are a number of recurring
messages throughout the various chapters. Our goals in this chapter are to
identify these messages, stress a few additional points, and offer some summary thoughts on where we in higher education go from here in addressing campus gambling.

Seven Messages

The first of the messages recurring throughout the volume is that campus
gambling is an issue that demands greater attention from all those concerned with student development and success, with the integrity of intercollegiate athletics and our institutions of higher education, and with the
health of our communities—campus and beyond. To do otherwise would
be to fail our students, our institutions, and our ethical obligations.

Second, just as we have learned with our work on other challenging
social issues, there are no simple solutions or universal templates for action.
It is essential in focusing our attention and efforts on campus gambling, just

NEW DIRECTIONS FOR STUDENT SERVICES, no. 113, Spring 2006 © Wiley Periodicals, Inc.
Published online in Wiley InterScience (www.interscience.wiley.com) • DOI: 10.1002/ss.199

as it is in our work on those other issues, that we do so in ways that are informed by our ethics and values (personal, professional, and institutional), applicable laws, institutional contexts, current research, and best practices. An example of a gambling-related project that we believe is consistent with this message and that may hold great promise is the work of the Center for College Health and Safety (CCHS) at the University of Massachusetts, Boston. At the request of the Massachusetts Department of Public Health, the CCHS (a department of the U.S. Department of Education's Higher Education Center for Alcohol and Other Drug Abuse and Violence Prevention) has submitted a proposal to work with several institutions in the state to collect data on campus gambling and develop, implement, and assess a data-driven comprehensive program campus gambling prevention program using a public health ecological framework (personal correspondence with Beth DeRicco, 2005).

The third message, and a natural extension of the second, is that we must undertake the research and scholarship of practice necessary to better understand the phenomena associated with campus gambling. Engaging in such research and scholarship requires the support of our institutions at the most senior levels. It will be important to keep in mind that some of what we discover may be unflattering data and difficult choices.

The fourth message relates to the challenges presented by what McClellan and Winters described earlier as the fourth wave of gambling. The various aspects of campus gambling are evolving and unfolding at a rapid rate. The fourth wave of gambling, driven by the Internet and explosive growth in gambling opportunities and participation, challenges us to constantly scan the environment for the latest developments and future developments.

Fifth, even though we must become engaged in addressing campus gambling, there is no reason to presume that doing so will require already hard-working (and sometimes overstretched) professionals to create a substantial number of new programs or to work significant additional hours. Opportunities to address campus gambling already exist in a variety of programmatic venues on our campuses. We should begin our work in this area with an eye toward those already existing opportunities.

The sixth message is a simple but important one. Campuses are best advised to be proactive in their approach to gambling education and intervention, not forced to be reactive to the negative consequences, minor or major, that may result from having neglected the issue. The NASPA white paper (McClellan and others, 2002), the framework suggested by Jason Laker in Chapter Seven, and the Gambling Action Team model shared by Chris King and Tom Hardy in Chapter Eight are all helpful resources for any campus wishing to be proactive in its approach to addressing campus gambling.

The seventh and final message is that addressing campus gambling requires a collaborative effort of students, staff, and faculty. Although the student affairs profession is ideally situated to facilitate campus consensus and action in this area, it would be a mistake for student affairs to assume or become saddled with the assignment of responding to campus gambling.

And a Few Points

There are several additional points that we wish to stress in this final chapter. First among these is the tendency we have observed on campuses reacting to gambling issues to address the behavior without considering the need to address the potential health issue. As an example, the student bookie at the center of the campus incident or scandal is likely to be a student who has gotten caught up in compulsive gambling behavior rather than a true businessperson involved in bookmaking. If problem or pathological gambling is at the heart of the person's actions, the student should be held accountable for the behavior and offered help in addressing the health issue.

Another point we wish to make is the need for the two major student affairs professional associations to identify areas in which they can partner with other higher education professional associations and intercollegiate associations to address campus gambling. To date, such cooperation has been largely lacking. Our collective shortfall in this area is dramatically illustrated by the absence of substantial student affairs involvement in the NCAA's Task Force on Gambling and the lack of references in the Reno Model (Blaszczynski, Ladouceur, and Shaffer, 2004, an important paper articulating a framework for addressing youth gambling) to student affairs professionals as potential key partners. It is unlikely that the associations will be in complete agreement with regard to best approaches to all aspects of campus gambling, but surely we can find substantial agreement in many areas.

The third and final point we wish to make in this section is the need for student affairs professionals, other higher education professionals, and institutions of higher education to critically examine their own involvement in gambling-related activities. Should we as individuals be involved in gambling? Should we use gambling as a programming alternative? Should we accept gambling-related revenues to support our programs or our institutions? If we believe that we should engage in any or all of these sorts of activities, what obligations are incumbent on us as a result? The authors of this chapter are not unanimous in their answers to these questions, but unanimous in the belief that it is critically important that these questions be addressed.

Where We Go From Here

Shaffer, Hall, Vander Bilt, and George (2003) note that this generation of students comes to campus at a time when gambling is largely socially acceptable and seen as a commonplace form of entertainment. We would add that, driven by the aggressive marketing of the gambling interests and media glamorization of the gambling lifestyle, an alarming number of our students see gambling as a means of financing their education or as a career field offering lucrative rewards and desirable working conditions.

Competing with well-financed and unrelenting media messages in an effort to engage students in self-reflection on whether or to what extent engaging in a behavior is consistent with their values and their future goals is not new to those of us working in student affairs. Where we have been effective in doing so, it is the result of our commitment to consistently engage students as adults able to make good choices when furnished with the information and support to do so.

It is difficult to argue with the observation that the gambling genie is out of the bottle, and it seems evident, given the genie's size and potential to change our lives, that we cannot simply ignore it. Instead, we must discover ways in which to learn and live with the genie present.

References

Blaszczynski, A., Ladouceur, R., and Shaffer, H. J. "A Science-Based Framework for Responsible Gambling: The Reno Model." *Journal of Gambling Studies,* 2004, *20.* http://www.ncrg.org/assets/files/Reno_Model_JGS_2004.pdf; accessed Oct. 18, 2005.

McClellan, G., Caswell, J., Beck, B., Graves-Holladay, C., Mitchell, A., and Wong-O'Connor, K. *Gambling, Its Effects and Prevalence on College Campuses: Implications for Student Affairs.* Washington, D.C.: National Association for Student Personnel Administrators, 2002.

Shaffer, H. J., Hall, M. N., Vander Bilt, J., and George, E. (eds.). *Futures at Stake: Youth, Gambling, and Society.* Reno: University of Nevada Press, 2003.

GEORGE S. MCCLELLAN *is vice president for student development at Dickinson State University; he served as lead author of NASPA's white paper on campus gambling and was cochair of NASPA's Gambling Task Force.*

JIM CASWELL *is vice president for student affairs at Southern Methodist University; he served as coauthor of NASPA's white paper on campus gambling and was cochair of NASPA's Gambling Task Force.*

THOMAS W. HARDY *is director of housing and residence life at Valdosta State University and previously served as cochair of the Gambling Action Team at the University of Alabama.*

RESOURCES

Links to Academic Centers

Center for Gaming Research
Comprehensive Web site with a rich array of well-maintained links. University of
Nevada, Las Vegas (http://gaming.unlv.edu).

Institute for the Study of Gambling and Commercial Gaming
Information on the gaming industry and issues affecting it. University of Nevada, Reno
(http://www.unr.edu/gaming/index.asp).

Institute for Research on Pathological Gambling and Related Disorders
Harvard Medical School, Division of Addictions. Includes links to research findings and
model programs (http://www.hms.harvard.edu/doa/institute/index.htm).

International Center for Youth Gambling Problems and High Risk Behaviors
McGill University. Comprehensive and well-maintained site focusing on youth gambling
(http://www.education.mcgill.ca/gambling).

Links to Journals and Research Studies

International Gambling Studies
Journal with international focus, available by subscription (http://www.tandf.co.uk/
journals/titles/14459795.asp).

Journal of Gambling Issues
A high-quality free e-journal (http://www.camh.net/egambling).

NEW DIRECTIONS FOR STUDENT SERVICES, no. 000, Fall 2005   © Wiley Periodicals, Inc.
Published online in Wiley InterScience (www.interscience.wiley.com) • DOI: 10.1002/ss.200

Journal of Gambling Studies
Journal with abstracts free and articles for fee or by subscription (http://www.ingenta-connect.com/content/klu/jogs).

The Wager
An online research bulletin dedicated to pathological gambling (http://www.basison-line.org/wager)

Links to Support Services

Gamblers Anonymous
Features a self-diagnostic survey regarding gambling behavior, an FAQ on compulsive gambling, and a list of Gamblers Anonymous chapters across the United States and around the world (http://www.gamblersanonymous.org).

National Council on Problem Gambling
Features a self-diagnostic survey regarding gambling behavior, an impressive array of links to gambling-related resources around the world, and a list of gambling help resources across the United States (http://www.ncpgambling.org).

The Council on Compulsive Gambling of New Jersey
Features a self-diagnostic survey regarding gambling behavior, articles of interest regarding gambling behavior, and a list of gambling help resources across the United States and Canada (http://www.800gambler.org).

INDEX

Back Issue/Subscription Order Form

Copy or detach and send to:

Jossey-Bass, A Wiley Imprint, 989 Market Street, San Francisco CA, 94103-1741

Call or fax toll-free: Phone 888-378-2537 6:30AM – 3PM PST; Fax 888-481-2665

Back Issues: Please send me the following issues at $27 each
(Important: please include ISBN number for each issue.)

_____

_____

_____

$ _____   Total for single issues

$ _____   SHIPPING CHARGES: SURFACE   Domestic Canadian
                                          First Item $5.00 $6.00
                                          Each Add'l Item $3.00 $1.50
                     For next-day and second-day delivery rates, call the number listed above.

Subscriptions   Please __ start __ renew my subscription to *New Directions for Student Services* for the year 2_____at the following rate:

U.S.   __ Individual $75   __ Institutional $180
Canada   __ Individual $75   __ Institutional $220
All Others   __ Individual $99   __ Institutional $254

**For more information about online subscriptions visit
www.wileyinterscience.com**

$ Total single issues and subscriptions (Add appropriate sales tax for your state for single issue orders. No sales tax for U.S. subscriptions. Canadian residents, add GST for subscriptions and single issues.)
_____

__Payment enclosed (U.S. check or money order only)

__VISA __ MC __ AmEx Card #_____Exp.Date_____

Signature ——————————————————————— Day Phone _____

__Bill Me (U.S. institutional orders only. Purchase order required.)

Purchase order # ————————————————————————
                  Federal Tax ID13559302   **GST 89102 8052**

Name _____

Address _____

_____

Phone _____ E-mail _____

For more information about Jossey-Bass, visit our Web site at www.josseybass.com

ERRATA

In issue no. 112 of New Directions for Student Services, *Technology in Student Affairs: Supporting Student Learning and Services,* one chapter author's name was inadvertently omitted.

Chapter 1, "Technology and Student Affairs: Redux," was co-authored by Caroline A. Nisbet, assistant vice president for student affairs at Duke University.

The publisher regrets the error and thanks Ms. Nisbet for her contributions.